A Chair for Yoga
A complete guide to Iyengar Yoga practice with a chair

by
Eyal Shifroni, Ph.D.

Second Edition

A Chair for Yoga

*A complete guide to Iyengar Yoga
practice with a chair*

Second Edition

by

Eyal Shifroni, Ph.D.

Based on the teachings of
Yogacharya B.K.S. Iyengar,
Geeta S. Iyengar, and Prashant S. Iyengar
at the
Ramamani Iyengar Memorial Institute (RIMYI),
Pune, India

Eyal Shifroni

A Chair for Yoga

A complete guide to Iyengar Yoga
practice with a chair

Table of Contents

Preface to the Second Edition

The first edition of this book was received very well by teachers and students of Yoga around the world. Since its publication in April 2013, many people responded with enthusiastic feedback; some even suggested certain variations of their own. I myself have conducted several workshops based on the book, where new ideas emerged. I tested the accumulated material and, having added some new variations, decided it is time to publish a second edition. I hope this new, expanded edition will trigger new ways of exploring the *asanas* in your practice!

Eyal Shifroni
November 2013

Acknowledgments and Gratitude

The source of all the knowledge presented in this guide is my Guru, Yogacharia B.K.S Iyengar, the founder of the Iyengar Yoga method. The use of chairs in Yoga practice was introduced by Mr. Iyenger along with many other tools that he has invented and adapted over the years. I wish to express my deep admiration and gratitude for him not only as my personal teacher, but also for making Yoga accessible to millions, enabling every person to benefit from the gift of Yoga. I wish also to thank my Guru, Mr. Iyengar, for devoting his precious time to reviewing the manuscript and suggesting valuable corrections. As always, his accurate suggestions proved immensely valuable, pushed me to re-take some of the photos and contributed to my confidence in publishing the guide.

My initial interest in writing this guide was kindled during visits to Pune while practicing with a chair under the guidance of Prashant Iyengar at RIMYI. Geeta Iyengar's DVD: "The role of the chair in the yogi's life" ignited many of the ideas presented in this guide.

I wish to thank these three great teachers for introducing me to the world of Iyengar Yoga and for being a continuous source of knowledge and inspiration!

I also wish to thank many other teachers, most notably Faeq Biria, Birjoo Mehta and Jawahar Bangera, who have deepened and enriched my practice, with and without chairs.

Gratitude is have also due to my students who helped test and develop new ideas involving the use of chairs during classes and workshops. I hope that they have enjoyed this process as much as me!

The writings of this guide have been a joint-project of all the teachers who teach with me at the center in Zichron-Ya'akov (Israel). We have all experimented and tried the chair-work with our students, and each has contributed his own ideas. I want to say thanks especially to:

❖ Michael Sela who went through my writings over and over with endless patience and edited the text. He helped me formulate this guide and to express my ideas more concisely and clearly.
❖ Ravit Moar and Rachel Hasson who spent many hours modeling for the photos in this guide.
❖ Kym Ben-Ya'akov for contributing her talents both as a Yoga teacher and as an American native English-speaker using her hawk-eye to check the English in this guide.

Thanks to Anat Scher for her willingness to model for the photos of the appendix. Special thanks also to my student Ram Amit who volunteered to take the photos and who did such a dedicated and wonderful job! Thanks also to my sweet daughter, Ayelet, who took some of the photos and edited all the photos to give them a final touch.

And, last but not least, I want to thank my wife, Hagit. Without her love and support, this guide (and many other things) could never have become real.

Photography: Ram Amit

Models: Ravit Moar, Rachel Hasson & Eyal Shifroni

Graphic Design: Einat Merimi | Studio A.N.A.

Text Editing: Michael Sela

Introduction

This guide is a modest attempt to present how a chair can be used to deepen and enhance the practice of *Yogasasna*. It was born out of the interest and enthusiasm expressed by my students during classes and workshops in which we explored various ways to use chairs. They requested me to document this work, so that they could continue to practice at home.

We hope that this presentation will help practitioners, students and teachers make systematic use of chairs in their practice, thus helping to spread Iyengar Yoga for the benefit of all!

The Use of Props

B.K.S. Iyengar has developed a range of equipment and accessories that enable every person to improve her/his *asana* practice and benefit from it. The main purposes of these "props" are to help the practitioner:

— Perform *asanas* which are difficult to perform independently
— Achieve and maintain correct alignment during the practice
— Stay longer and relax in challenging *asanas*, in order to attain their full benefit
— Study and investigate the *asanas* in greater depth.

Props are indeed an important characteristic of Iyengar Yoga, but they should not be confused with its essence. Props are a means to an end - such as alignment, stability, precision, and staying longer in *asanas*.

This guide focuses on one such prop: the chair! It contains eight chapters, each dedicated to another family of *asanas*, and an appendix "A chair for all – a gentle practice sequence".

The usages of the chair covered here, are intended to direct awareness to different aspects of the *asanas* and to different parts of the body, in order to deepen and enhance the understanding of the *asanas*. Practitioners should be careful not to develop dependency on props; rather, props should be employed intelligently in pursuit of a more mature and mindful *asanas* practice.

What Type of Chairs Should be Used?

The chair must be stable and sturdy and have a horizontal, square-shaped, flat seat at the appropriate height (about a 45 cm elevation from the floor). It is strongly recommended to use the folding metal chairs used in RIMYI and other Iyengar centers. These chairs are typically equipped with two horizontal, supportive metal rungs, one welded between the front legs and the other between the rear legs. The backs of such chairs should be removed, in order to expose the frame of the backrest for ease of gripping and for enabling movement through it.

Important Notes

1. This guide is not intended for people suffering from special health problems. If you suffer from a severe health problem, please seek guidance from a teacher who is certified to conduct therapeutic Yoga classes.

2. This guide is not intended for newcomers, but for people who have already acquired some basic knowledge and are familiar with the basic techniques of the presented *asanas*. For a complete guide on the techniques of *asanas*, please refer to *Light on Yoga* by B.K.S Iyengar, or other sources such as *Yoga – the Path to Holistic Health* by the same author. *Yoga in Action* by Gita S. Iyengar is a recommended introduction to Yoga practice.

3. The techniques shown here are based on the insights and principles of the Iyengar method. Using the props without understanding these principles misses the point. Our motivation is to facilitate and deepen the understanding of these principles. For this reason, a practitioner using this guide should have a solid foundation in Iyengar Yoga.

4. For some of the advanced (and less familiar) poses, we have added a reference to the plate depicting the pose in *Light on Yoga*; for example, for *Bhujangasana II* (shown in plate 550) we added the reference: LOY, Pl. 550.

5. Finally, remember that no guide can include <u>all</u> the options of chair use in Yoga. We encourage you to practice in a playful manner; to explore, invent and discover other ways of enhancing your Yoga practice with a chair! For comments and suggestions please write to the author at **eyal@theiyengaryoga.com.**

CAUTION!

Users of this guide must have a solid foundation in Yoga practice, preferably obtained through regular classes with a certified Iyengar Yoga teacher. Some of the variations shown in this guide are advanced and should not be attempted without guidance and supervision. The author takes no responsibility for any injury or damage that may occur due to improper use of the material presented.

Enjoy your practice!

Chapter 1: Standing Asanas - Utthitha Sthiti

Tadasana or Samashtiti

In *Tadasana*, the chair gives a sense of direction and helps to achieve correct alignment.

We show three ways of using the chair.

Variation 1: Chair behind

A chair placed behind helps to roll the shoulders back:

- ➲ Turn the chair backwards and stand in front of it, your back facing the backrest.
- ➲ Stand in *Tadasana* and place the fingers on top of the backrest.
- ➲ Use the support of the hands to extend the spine and open the chest.
- ➲ Use the backrest as a gauge for the vertical alignment.

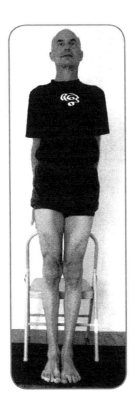
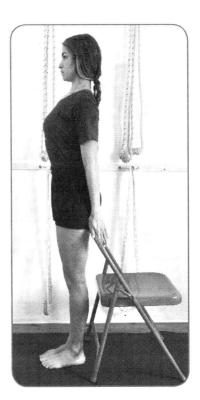

Variation 2: Chair in front

A chair placed in front helps to lift the chest and to check the lateral alignment.

The support of the chair, gentle as it is, helps to align and balance the pose and to make it even (*sama*).

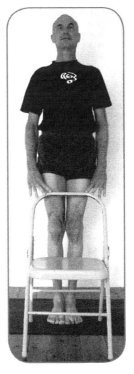

Variation 3: Toe mounds on the chair legs

Lifting the toe mounds elongates the calf muscles and the Achilles' tendons. This is especially useful for joggers and cyclists, whose activity tends to shorten these muscles. It is important to stretch and massage these muscles as dilated calf muscles indicate accumulation of venous blood, which slows down the circulation.

Variation 3 can also be used in *Urdhva Hastasana.* ⇨

Adho Mukha Svanasana

Raising the palm support in *Adho Mukha Svanasana* (downward facing dog) helps to shift the body weight to the legs and stay longer in the pose. In this way, even beginners can practice this important *asana* and learn to work the legs, extend the trunk, open the chest, and so on.

Variation 1: Raising the palms

The following sequence presents three stages of moving into the pose, using the chair to raise the hands and provide resistance for the hands.

Stage 1: Palms on seat
- ⮑ Place the chair with its seat against the wall.
- ⮑ Place the palms on the seat and step back into the pose ❶.

The high support for the hands is very useful for people who are stiff or have weak arms. It helps to shift the body weight from the arms to the legs.

Stage 2: Palms on rung
- ⮑ Now turn the chair so that its front faces the wall. Place the base of each palm against the rung of the chair.
- ⮑ Open the palms and spread the fingers apart ❷.

Note that in stage 2, the force you apply on the chair may fold it. To prevent this, place the chair with its seat facing the wall. In this way, the chair will slide and fold slightly until it is stopped by the wall. Then, it will not fold anymore and you will be able to lean safely on it.

Stage 3: Palms on floor

- ➲ If possible, take the hands further down and place the palms on the floor.
- ➲ Place the chair's legs between the index and thumb of the corresponding hand.
- ➲ Spread the fingers well while pushing against the chair legs ❸.

Variation 2: Chair inverted

The chair can also be used when placed upside down to support the palms or the feet.

i. Palms support

- ➲ Turn the chair upside down and place its backrest against the wall.
- ➲ Place the palms on the bottom side of the seat (or hold the legs of the chair).
- ➲ Step back into the pose.

Pushing the palms against a slanted surface helps to lift the forearms and tighten the elbows. In addition, the legs of the chair support the forearms and elbows. This is very relaxing for the arms and it is a boon for people who tend to hyper-extend the elbows.

People with a wide shoulder girdle are advised to hold the legs of the chair instead of placing the palms against the seat. This helps to roll the arms from inside out (move the triceps muscles closer to the center line and the biceps muscles away from the center line of the body).

The same placement of the chair can be used in *Adho Mukha Virasana* as shown here:

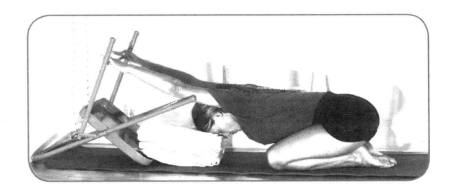

ii. Feet support
It is also possible to place the feet on the slanted seat.

Placing the feet higher lifts the buttock bones and sharpens the awareness in the pelvic girdle. Press the heels down in order to get the full extension of the legs.

More on the use of the inverted chair will be presented later.

Variation 3: Leaning on the chair

In this variation, the front side of the torso leans on the chair. The heels are lifted and supported against the wall. It is recommended to place blankets on top of the backrest and the seat in order to soften the contact points ❶.

This variation is very useful for releasing and extending the back, especially after practicing backbends. It gives rest and extension to the entire body. The abdomen is broadened and recedes toward the lower back.

If needed, blocks can be used to support the palms and/or feet ❷.

Ardha Uttanasana

Ardha (half) *Uttanasana* prepares for *Uttanasana* and *Adho Mukha Svanasana*. Beginners, who find it difficult to bend from the pelvis, bending instead from the lumbar region, are advised to practice this pose before attempting full *Uttanasana*. Bending from the lumbar is unsafe as it compresses the vertebra in this region; hence, the use of the chair.

Variation 1: Outer wrists on the backrest

➲ Stand at the appropriate distance from the chair, stretch the arms up to *Urdhva Hastasana* and then bend forward. Place the outer wrists on the backrest of the chair, palms facing each other. Move the front thighs back and stretch the trunk forward ❶.

This easy variation helps to train the legs by lifting the arches and the kneecaps; opening the back of the knees; turning the upper thighs in, etc. It also helps to stretch the back and make it concave.

Variation 2: Chin on the backrest

Lifting and supporting the chin enables one to concave the back and provides further extension to the front spine and neck.

Note:
Before arching the neck, be sure to extend the spine forward, concave it, and move the trapezius muscle away from the neck. This prevents compression of the neck vertebras ❷.

Variation 3: Resting the forehead on the bolster

Resting the forehead on a soft support enables deep relaxation for the brain ❸.

Variation 4: Resting on the backrest

- ⮑ Stand facing the backrest of the chair and spread the legs apart until the front groins reach the height of the backrest (use a blanket for cushioning).
- ⮑ Bend forward and use the support of the backrest to extend the trunk forward ❶.
- ⮑ Lower the head and place the forehead on the seat. You can comfortably hold the chair legs and relax ❷.

Tall people should spread their legs further apart, thus making the pose similar to *Prasarita Padottanasana* ❸.

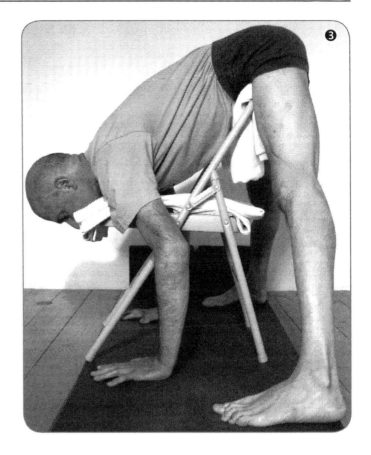

Variation 5: Opening the shoulders

A helper can provide traction to create movement and opening in the shoulders.

➲ The helper sits on the chair. The practitioner bends forward to *Ardha Uttanasana*, places his/her shoulders on the helper's thighs, interlocks the fingers with arms stretched behind his/her back and hooks the palms around the helper's neck.

➲ The helper gently pushes the practitioner's shoulder blades in (toward the floor) while moving the skin of the upper back toward the middle back, and leans backward to provide traction to the shoulders.

Note:

As in all cases when assisting, the helper should be sensitive and alert not to overstretch the practitioner.

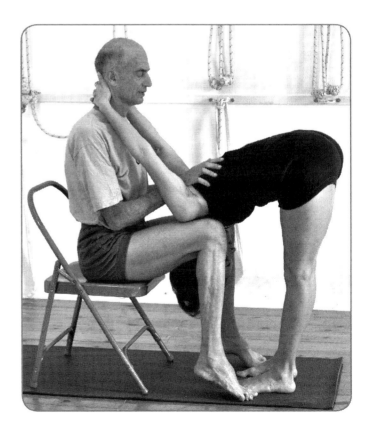

Uttanasana

This is an intense stretch for the entire back side of the body. The chair can be used for relaxing the pose and extending its duration. Three such variations are shown below, each with a unique effect. The forth variation demonstrates how the chair may be used to increase the stretch.

Variation 1: Head resting on the seat

Placing the forehead or the crown of the head on the seat provides deep relaxation for the brain and the eyes ❶.

Variation 2: Shoulder girdle on the seat

This variation requires greater flexibility.

➲ Stand in front of the chair, bend into *Uttanasana* and place the back of the shoulder girdle against the edge of the seat ❷ ❸.

The slight pressure on the base of the neck releases the neck muscles.

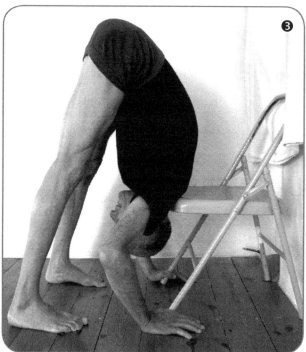

Variation 3: Front groins against the backrest

- ⮑ Fold the chair and lean the backrest against the front groins. Adjust the height by tilting the chair to the desired angle.

- ⮑ Bend forward, hold the legs of the chair, make the back concave and look forward ❶.
- ⮑ Now, exhale and bend into the final pose ❷.

The touch of the backrest on the front thighs helps to keep the groins high, creating space in the pelvic region and maintaining the horizontal symmetry of the pose.

Taller practitioners will need to hold the chair at a steeper angle ❸.

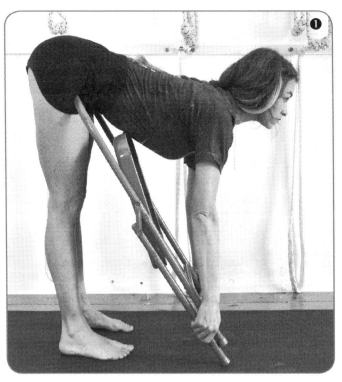

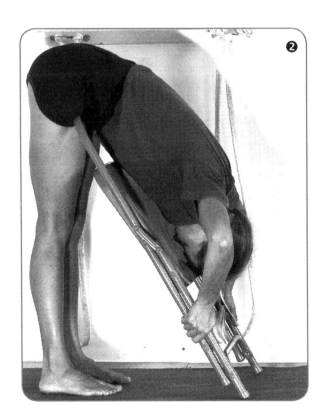

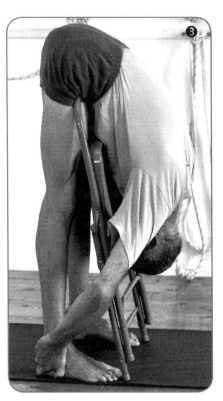

Variation 4: Standing on the seat

This variation facilitates a more intense stretch.

- ➲ Stand on the seat facing the front. Releae the toes over the edge. Spread the legs to pelvis width.
- ➲ Bend forward and hold the seat or the front legs of the chair.
- ➲ Use the arms to pull and increase the stretch.

 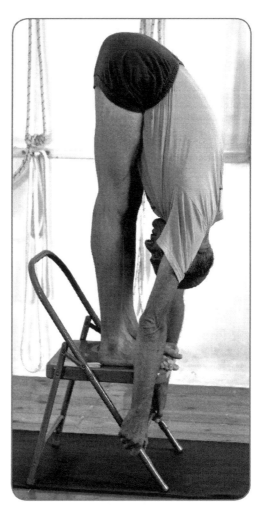

The chair provides a grip for the hands, thus making the arms much more effective in creating a stretch for the back body.

When one stands at a height, a fear of falling may arise. This variation helps to overcome such fear, and to develop balance, stability and confidence.

The following examples show the use of chairs for support and stability in several standing *asanas*, thus enabling one to stay longer in the pose and place more attention to finer details of the pose. It also enables stiff people to enjoy these poses. Generally speaking, the chair can be used in three ways: behind, in front or inverted.

Utthita Trikonasana

Utthita Trikonasana (Triangle pose) is a basic standing pose. The chair can help in finding the correct alignment of the pose and in extending its duration with reduced effort.

Variation 1: Chair behind

To use the chair on the right side:

- Place the chair behind you on the right side with the seat facing backwards (the backrest closer to you).
- Turn the right leg out and hold the backrest behind the back with the left hand ❶.
- Bend into the pose and place the right hand on the seat ❷.
- Using the grip of the left hand on the backrest, open the chest and turn it upward ❸.
- If possible, go further down and grip the leg of the chair or the horizontal rung close to the floor ❹.

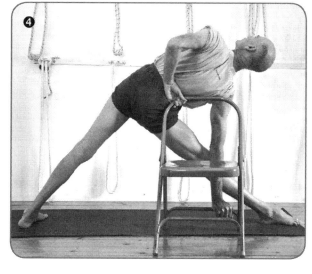

This variation, where the chair is behind, helps to move the shoulders back – especially the left shoulder (back leg shoulder) - and to turn the chest upward.

A helper can give traction to the spine and neck ❺.

Variation 2: Chair in front

This variation is helpful when there is difficulty in reaching the ankle of the front leg.

To use the chair on the left side:

➲ Place the chair in front of you and align the left side of the chair with the left leg.

➲ Turn the left leg out.

➲ Go into the pose, place the left hand on the seat and hold the backrest with the right hand. Push the right hand to turn the chest.

The chair supports and stabilizes the pose and helps to broaden the pelvis and turn the chest upward.

Variation 3: Foot on the inverted chair

Here, the chair is turned upside down and the front foot is supported on the slanted bottom of the seat.

To use the chair on the right side:

↪ Invert the chair (legs up) and place the backrest against the wall.

↪ Turn the right leg out and place the foot on the inverted seat ❶.

↪ Go into the pose and hold the higher horizontal rung. You can turn the palm out as in ❷. This helps to roll the shoulder back and turn the chest upward.

↪ If possible, go down further and hold the lower horizontal rung, next to the right leg ❸.

A back view is shown in ❹.

The slanted support of the front foot activates the front leg and helps to shift the body weight to the back leg. This variation is a good workout for the joints of the front leg: the ankle, the knee and the hip. It strengthens the knee and helps to move the head of the femur (thigh bone) into its socket in the pelvic girdle.

The rungs of the chair provide hand support at two levels: a higher one (to start with) and a lower one (to move deeper into the pose).

Variation 4: Foot on the seat

Placing the front foot higher increases the effect of the previous variation.

To do the pose on the left side:

⮕ Place the chair with its back against the wall.

⮕ Place the middle of the left heel against the edge of the seat and bend into the pose.

This variation further reduces the load on the front leg. The pressure of the heel on the edge of the seat activates the foot, knee and hip of the front leg. The knee becomes active without overloading it, and the femur bone is drawn better into the socket of the hip joint. The back leg (right in photo) becomes heavy and stable.

The same placement of the front foot can be applied to other standing poses. Try it in *Parsvottanasana, Parivrtta Trikonasana, Virabhadrasana II, Utthita Parsvakonasana* and *Parivrtta Parsvakonasana*. (Only *Parivrtta Trikonasana will be shown here*).

Virabhadrasana II

This is an intense pose and a good stretch for the inner legs and groins.

Variation 1: Resting the buttock on the seat

In this variation, the chair is used to support the buttock of the front leg.

To use the chair on the right side:

⊃ Place the chair in front of you and align the front edge of the seat with the right leg.

⊃ Turn the right leg out and pull the chair into the space between your legs ❶.

⊃ Bend the right leg and place the chair seat to support the right buttock. (You will have to move the chair a little to the right as you bend the leg).

⊃ Keep the left leg well stretched.

⊃ Hold the backrest and use the arms to turn the chest from right to left, and to lift it upward ❷.

The chair takes the load off the right leg. This enables one to stay in the pose using less effort and to work on the details of the pose, such as stretching the left leg and moving it backwards; rolling the right knee out and making sure it is bent to 90⁰; creating width in the pelvis; lifting the lower abdomen; and turning the chest from right to left.

Positioning the seat between the two thighs helps to spread the legs and open the groins.

⊃ If the chair is lower than the bottom of your knee, place a folded blanket or a foam block on the seat ❸.

The chair can also be placed behind.
This helps to roll the shoulders back ❹.

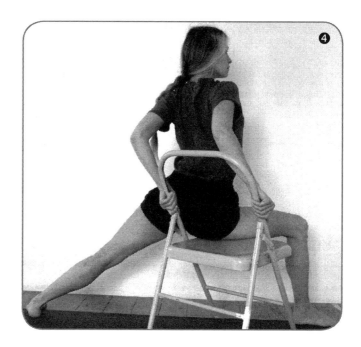

Variation 2: Foot on the inverted chair
In this variation, the foot of the front leg
is raised and placed on the slanted surface
of the inverted chair. The instructions
on how to use the chair and the effects
of this variation are explained in *Utthita
Trikonasana* (see page 14).

Utthita Parsvakonasana

Variation 1: Buttock on the seat

As in *Virabhadrasana II*, here the chair can be used to support the buttock of the front leg. This has similar effects and enables concentration on the stretch with the reduced load.

Gripping the chair in front helps to roll the chest up ❶.

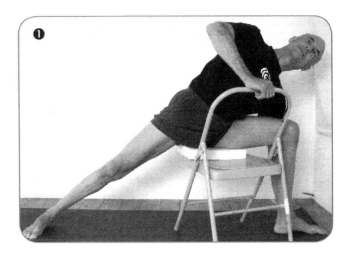

Gripping the chair from behind helps to roll the upper shoulder back (left shoulder in ❷ and ❸). The chair also helps to turn the chest up.

Another option is to turn the chair and insert the front leg under the backrest ❹.

When doing the pose on the right (as in ❹), the chair supports the right armpit, helping to maintain the length of the right waist (which tends to shrink in this pose).

Variation 2: Foot ont the inverted chair

In this variation, the foot of the front leg is raised and placed on the slanted surface of the inverted chair. Instructions on how to use the chair and the effects of this variation are given in *Utthita Trikonasana* (see page 14).

Virabhadrasana I

This is a challenging pose which requires flexibility and strength. The chair can be used to support the front leg's buttock, thus making the pose lighter. It enables one to stay in the pose longer and to concentrate on the back leg.

Variation 1: To use the chair on the right side:

- ➲ Stand facing the chair and insert the right leg under the backrest.
- ➲ Bend the right leg to 90⁰ and place the right buttock on the chair ❶. If needed, place a folded blanket or foam block on the seat to adjust the height ❸.
- ➲ Lift the right heel and turn the leg and the pelvis from left to right.
- ➲ Move the left buttock away from the tail bone and the front left groin forward to touch the seat ❷.

A side view of the pose done on the left is shown in ❷.

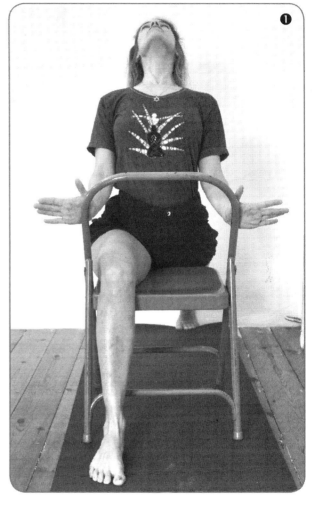

Holding the backrest helps to lift the chest and brings it to the correct alignment, which is right above the pelvis and facing forward. Lifting the chest helps to lift the whole torso from the pubic bone and up ❶.

Pushing the left heel against the wall, as shown on the previous page ❸, helps to turn the pelvis to the front and to maintain the stretch of the back leg. Gradually, with practice, the front groins will lengthen making this rather difficult action possible.

Variation 2: In this variation, the chair is used solely for supporting the hands:
⮑ Place the chair in front with the backrest facing you.
⮑ Bend into the pose and hold the backrest.

To help turning the left leg further in, place the heel against the wall.

This variation is closer to the final pose; holding the chair helps to lift and turn the chest and to roll the shoulders back.

Ardha Chandrasana

Ardha Chandrasana (Half-moon pose) is a balancing pose with many beneficial effects. It develops balance and strength, helps to keep the hip joints healthy and creates space in the pelvis (which is a boon for women during menstruation and pregnancy). Using the chair, one can maintain the required balance, achieve the correct alignment and stay longer.

Placement of the chair in front of the body provides support and a reference plane, which helps to balance in the pose and turn the chest up ❶.

Another recommended variation is to place the chair behind the body. To perform the pose on the left side:

- ➲ Place the chair behind you, aligned with the left leg, backrest against the left hip.
- ➲ Bend the left leg (the standing leg) and hold the back rung of the chair with the left hand (if the rung is too low, grip the leg of the chair.).
- ➲ Lift and stretch the right leg while stretching the left leg.
- ➲ Swing the right hand back and catch the backrest behind the back ❷.

A rear view of the pose done on the right is shown in ❸. This variation gives a good feel for correct alignment and also provides support for the lower shoulder (left in ❷). The support of the top arm (right arm in ❷) behind the back helps to open that shoulder and to turn the chest.

Parivrtta Trikonasana

This pose requires flexibility, balance, stability and spatial orientation.

Variation 1: Twisting to face the chair

In this variation, the chair provides a fulcrum for the twist and helps to keep balance. It also provides support for the hand when one has difficulty reaching the floor.

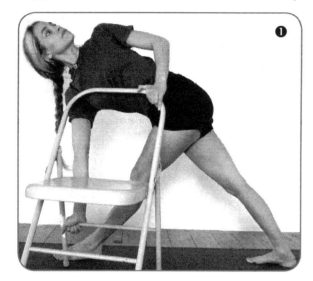

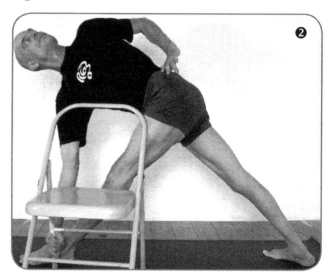

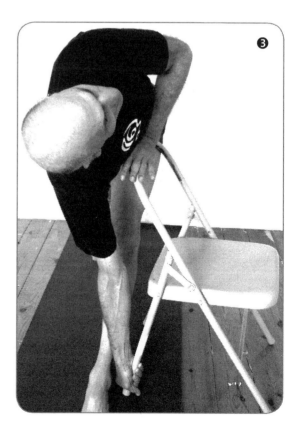

To use the chair on the left side:

- ⮑ Spread the legs and place the chair behind you near the left leg, backrest facing your back.
- ⮑ Turn the legs to the left. Extend the body to the left while twisting the torso until the chest is facing the chair.
- ⮑ With the right hand, catch the lower back rung of the chair (if you cannot reach it, simply place the palm on top of the seat) while the left hand holds and pushes the backrest ❶.
- ⮑ With each exhalation use the support of the chair to increase the twist, The left hand can be moved to the waist ❷, or stretched up as in the final pose.

   A view from the head side is shown in ❸.

Be sure to start with the chair behind you, so that after twisting you will be facing the chair.

Variation 2: Foot on the inverted chair

In this variation, the foot of the front leg is placed on the slanted surface of the inverted chair. The instructions on how to use the chair and the effects of this variation are explained in *Utthita Trikonasana* (see page 14).

This variation is especially helpful for *Parivrtta Trikonasana*, as it provides various support points for the lower arm (the right arm in the photos). You can catch the horizontal rung ❶, or the leg of the chair at any height. Gradually, you can lower the hand further down to catch the lower (front) leg of the chair ❷.

Variation 3: Foot on the seat

The foot of the front leg can be placed even higher, on the seat:

A similar variation was shown for *Utthita Trikonasana* (see page 16); here it is even more helpful as it shifts weight to the heel of the back leg – a challenging action in this pose.

Parivrtta Ardha Chandrasana

In this pose, the chair can be used either at the front or at the back.

To use the chair at the back, start by placing it in front, then twist and catch the chair behind the back.

To practice the pose on the left side:

◔ Spread the legs and place the chair in front of the body, backrest aligned with the left leg.

◔ Turn the legs and enter the pose on the left side.

◔ With the right hand, catch the horizontal rung, then swing the left hand and shoulder back to catch the backrest behind the body.

◔ The right foot can be placed against the wall to increase balance and provide resistance for the upper leg.

Parivrtta Parsvakonasana

This is an advanced twisting pose. The chair can help to prepare for the final pose, providing a stable fulcrum for the twist.

Variation 1: Twisting to face the chair
In this variation, the bent leg rests on the seat; hence, the effort to hold the pose is reduced and that leg is stabilized.

To use the chair on the left side:

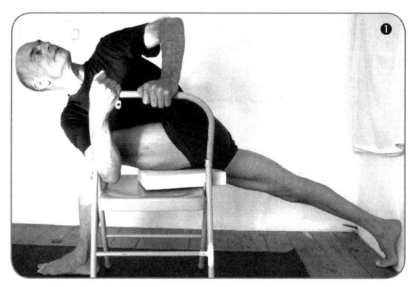

⮑ Stand with the right leg near the wall. Spread the legs and place the chair behind you, near the left leg, backrest facing away from you.

⮑ Bend the left leg to 90⁰ and place the left buttock on the chair (if you are tall, place a folded blanket or a foam block on the seat as in ❶).

⮑ Turn the right leg, lift the heel and place it on the wall. Twist the trunk from right to left until the chest is facing the chair.

⮑ Move the right armpit toward the left knee, bend the elbow, and catch the backrest.

⮑ With the left hand, hold the backrest from above, and push.

⮑ With each exhalation, use the support of the chair to increase the twist ❶ ❷.

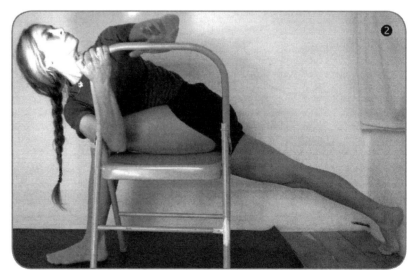

Variation 2: Foot on inverted chair

In this variation, the foot of the front leg is raised and placed on the slanted surface of the inverted chair. The instructions on how to use the chair are explained in the section on *Utthita Trikonasana* (see page 14).

Holding the leg of the chair and pushing the foot against the slanted surface helps to anchor the arm for the twist. This helps maintain stability and increase the movement in this challenging pose.

Virabhadrasana III

This pose is probably the most challenging standing *asana* with respect to strength and stability. For most beginners, it is quite difficult to hold the pose with correct alignment without supporting the hands.

Variation 1: Outer wrist on backrest

To use the chair on the right side:

⮑ Place the chair at an appropriate distance from you, the backrest facing you. Bend to *Ardha* (half) *Uttanasana* and place the outer wrists on the backrest. If the hips are higher than the backrest, put a folded blanket on the backrest or place the chair on blocks to increase its height.

⮑ At this stage, the legs are perpendicular and the torso and arms create a straight horizontal line.

⮑ Lift the left leg until it is horizontal and stretch it backwards, keeping the center of gravity right above the front of the heel of the standing foot (you can place the left foot against the wall to increase the stretch and get further support).

⮑ Press the wrists against the backrest to sink the shoulder blades into the body while lifting the inner arms and elbows.

Variation 2: Standing on the chair and holding the backrest

The backrest can support the hands also in another interesting way. To do the pose on the right leg:

↪ Stand on top of the seat facing the back of the chair.

↪ Bend to half *Uttanassana* and catch the backrest. To increase the outer turning of the shoulders you can turn the hands as in ❶.

↪ Move the front thighs back and extend the trunk forward. Look forward.

↪ Now lift the left leg until it is parallel to the floor. Extend the leg back and keep extending the trunk forward ❷.

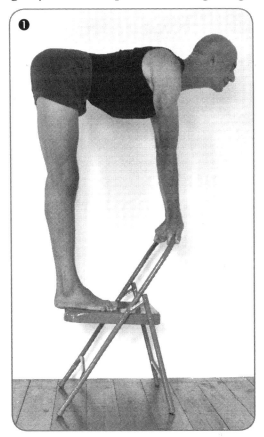

Parsvottanasana

In this pose, the chair can be used both for support and for checking the alignment of the pelvis.

Variation 1: Chair as a support

Use the support of the chair for stability in order to study the work of the legs and the turning of the pelvis. Beginners may find it hard to bend forward and place the hands on the floor; the support of the chair helps them stay in the pose. Practitioners who are able to reach the floor may still use this variation in order to improve the rotation of the pelvis.

To use the chair on the right side:

⮑ Place the chair in front of you. Move the left leg backward.

⮑ Inhale and extend the arms up then exhale and bend forward.

⮑ Place the outer wrists on the backrest. Look forward and concave the back ❶.

⮑ Now, bend further and lower the forehead until it rests on the seat ❷.

A bolster can be placed on the seat for cushioning and relaxation ❸.

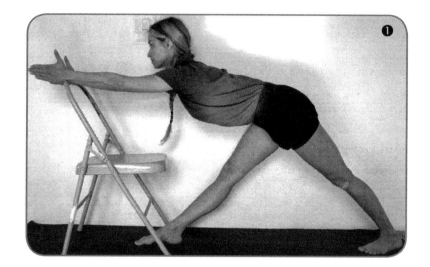

Variation 2: Chair to ensure alignment

In this variation, the chair is placed against the front groins, enabling one to check that the pelvis is sufficiently rotated. It also helps to keep the groins at an even height when bending forward.

To use the chair with the left leg forward:

⮑ Fold the chair and hold it in front with the seat facing up. Step backward with the right leg.

⮑ Place the backrest against the front groins. Make sure that the right groin touches the chair as much as the left one.

⮑ Bend half way forward and hold the legs of the chair. Concave the back and look forward ❶.

⮑ Exhale, bend further down and place the forehead on the chair. Keep rotating the right hip forward to touch the backrest with the right side ❷.

A bolster can be placed on the chair for cushioning and relaxation ❸.

Variation 3: Foot on the inverted chair

In this variation the foot of the front leg is raised and placed on the slanted surface of the inverted chair.

To use the chair on the right side:

⮑ Invert the chair and place its backrest against the wall (legs facing up).

⮑ Stand in front of the chair. Step forward with the right leg and place the foot on the (back surface of) seat.

⮑ Inhale, raise the arms up, extend the trunk and then bend forward and hold the back legs of the chair (see ❶).

⮑ Concave the back and look forward ❶.

⮑ Exhale and bend further to catch the front legs of the chair. Look forward and extend the front part of the spine ❷.

⮑ Now, bend and extend further forward, and lower the forehead to the shin ❸.

The chair helps to stay in the intermediate (concave back) stage ❷. This stage is important for learning how to extend the spine forward. Women during prganncy or menstruation should practice this stage only, and not bend all the way down. The support of the chair enables them to stay at this stage, while keeping their abdomen long, wide and soft.

As explained earlier, the placement of the foot on the slant improves the work of the front leg.

Prasarita Padottanasana I

A good way to work on this pose is with the back legs against the wall. This teaches the alignment of the legs (buttock bones and heels aligned on the same vertical plane) and the activation of the front thighs. Working with the wall, one tends to tilt forward and the chair can support the hands to prevent this. The chair also helps to lengthen the front body, concave the back and work on lifting the knee caps and flattening the front thighs toward the wall.

- Place the chair about 1 meter (3.5 feet) away from the wall with its seat facing the wall.
- Stand with the back to the wall and bend forward.
- Place the palms on the seat. If possible, bend further until the forearms touch the seat.
- Push the front thighs backward against the wall. Extend the torso forward, concave the back, and look forward ❶.

For a longer and more relaxed stay in the pose, a bolster can be placed on the chair to support the forehead. This variation is very helpful for women during menstruation and pregnancy ❷.

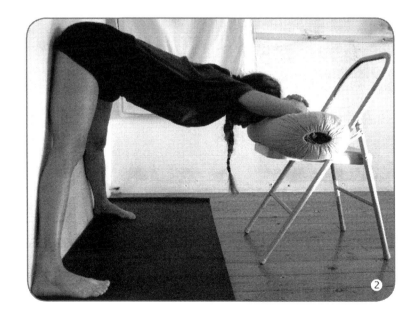

Utthita Hasta Padangusthasana II (lateral)

The work with the chair and the back against the wall makes this advanced pose accessible for everybody. The pose opens the pelvis, broadens the abdomen and can be used to prepare for *Utthita Trikonasana* and *Ardha Chandrasana*.

To use the chair on the left side:

⮑ Stand with your back to the wall and place the chair on the left side with the seat facing you. Place a piece of sticky mat on top of the backrest.

⮑ Bend the left leg and place the foot on the seat. Rotate the left knee out (toward the wall) and move the left buttock in (away from the wall). Stretch the right leg, moving the front thigh backwards toward the wall ❶.

⮑ Now loop a belt around the left foot, straighten the leg, and place the heel on the (cushioned) backrest ❷.

 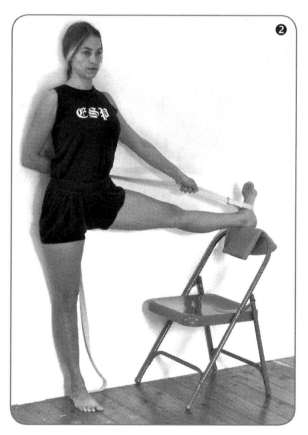

Staying with the support of the chair enables one to work on the delicate details of this pose (e.g. stretching the legs, moving the left buttock in, and keeping the *Tadasana* actions in the standing leg and in the torso).

Utthita Hasta Padangusthasana I (forward)

In this pose, place the chair in front of you to support the lifted leg. Hold the foot with a belt.

Make sure that the two sides of the pelvis are aligned (same height and same distance from the chair) ❶.

If possible, extend forward, hold the backrest and pull it to bend over the lifted leg ❷ (to approach the final pose, see LOY Pl. 23).

Utkatasana

In *Light on Yoga* B.K.S. Iyengar writes: "*Utkata* means powerful, fierce, uneven. This *asana* is like sitting on an imaginary chair." However, a real chair can still be used to help you bend deeply and stay longer in the pose:

- Stand in *Tadasana* and place the chair behind you.
- Lift the arms to *Urdhva Hastasana* or *Urdhva Namskarasana*.
- Bend the legs slightly, roll the flesh of the buttocks down and in. Slowly bend the legs further until you gently sit on the chair.
- Take a few breaths maintaining the stretch of the arms and torso and then slowly straighten the knees back to *Urdhva Hastasana*.
- Repeat several times.

This pose strengthens the quadriceps and is therefore important for the health of the knees. The chair helps to study the correct movement of coming into and out of the pose; it also helps to stay longer in the pose.

Garudasana

The challenge of this pose is to entwine the legs without losing the balance. Sitting on a chair helps to learn this.

- ➲ Sit on the chair and entwine the legs and arms.
- ➲ Once you can do the pose sitting, try to rise from the seat and hold the pose without supporting the buttocks.

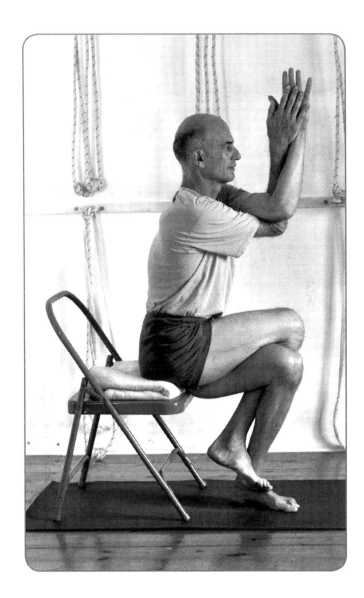

Vasisthasana

This is a balancing pose (LOY, Pl. 398); the chair helps to learn the pose and stay in it, so that you can work on stretching and opening the lifted leg.

To do the pose with the left leg lifted:

➲ Place the chair with the seat facing you and lie with your right side on the chair so that the right hip is supported by the edge of the seat.

➲ Enter the first stage of the pose by placing the right palm on the floor and stretching the left arm up ❶.

➲ Now, hold the big toe of the right leg with the right hand and stretch that leg vertically up ❷.

Chapter 2: Sitting Asanas - Upavistha Sthiti

In many of the sitting *asanas* the chair can be used to support the back. This helps to maintain the back upright, long and stable; to lift and open the chest; and to stay in the *asana* comfortably for an extended period of time.

Baddha Konasana

Variation 1: Supporting the back

Start by sitting high on the chair. This makes it easier to extend the spine upward and to open the chest.

- Sit on the chair and bring your feet together. If needed, prepare a folded blanket under the chair to support the buttocks when coming down. The blanket should be placed slightly forward ❶.
- Move the hips slightly forward and then slide down toward the floor. Support the back by pushing the palms against the seat ylwols so as to maintain the length of the torso ❷.

⮕ Finally, move the buttocks slightly back and sit on the blanket with the back supported against the front edge of the seat ❸ ❹.

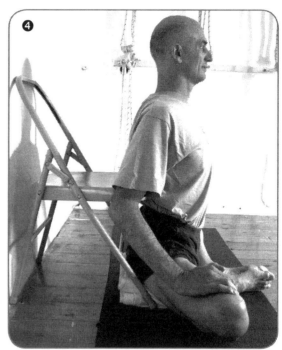

In many sitting poses, the support can be used for sitting upright as shown above (in Sanskrit this is called *Samaashrayi*). It can also be used for arching backwards to lift and open the chest further (this is called *Upaashrayi*).

⮕ To arch the back, raise the torso slightly and hold the backrest. Place a bolster or two on the seat to support the back of the head.

⮕ If you do not reach the backrest, loop a belt around the backrest and hold it ❺.

Help in *Baddha Konasana*

People who are flexible in the groins and inner thighs can get a further opening with the help of a teacher or another person. The helper sits on the chair, places his feet on the practitioner's thighs and gently presses them and rolls them out. The practitioner rests his arms on the helper's thighs to support the lifting of the trunk ❻.

Attention: The muscles of the groins are gentle so the helper should also be very gentle and take special care not to place too much weight on the practitioner's thighs. Do this variation only if you know the pose well and are aware of your limitations.

Using the chair as a backrest can be useful for other sitting poses like *Upavistha Konasana*, *Dandasana*, *Virasana* and *Sukhasana* (or *Swastikasana*) and *Padmasana*. In some of these asanas, however, it is not possible to descend from the chair as shown in *Baddha Konasana*.

Variation 2: Holding the chair

Here the chair helps to lift the chest and also induces stability and quietness.

Variation 3: Belt around the chest, blocks against the shins

A further opening of the chest, as well as spreading of the groins, can be achieved by hooking a belt to the backrest of the chair.

- ➲ Sit in *Baddha Konasana* facing the back of the chair. To stabilize the chair, place a heavy object on the seat, or ask someone to sit on it.

- ➲ Place two blocks between the shins and the legs of the chair.

- ➲ Place an open belt behind your mid-back, loop it around the backrest of the chair and adjust it so that it will support the back and move the chest forward and up.

- ➲ If possible, move the pelvis forward (closer to the chair) to get further opening of the groins and thighs.

Here, the chair serves two important purposes: first, the pull of the belt helps to open the chest and create space in the abdominal and the chest cavities; second, the pressure of the blocks helps to spread the bent legs and move them further back. These are basic actions in this pose.

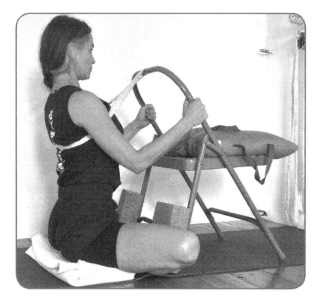

Upavistha Konasana

Variation 1: Supporting the back

○ Sit on the chair placed with its back against the wall and spread the legs wide.

○ Move the hips slightly forward and start sliding down ❶. See page 37 for detailed instructions.

○ Finally, sit on the floor (or on a folded blanket) and lean against the seat ❷.

○ Once seated, lift yourself and arch back to catch the backrest (with or without a belt) ❸. For staying longer, place two bolsters to support the back of the head ❸.

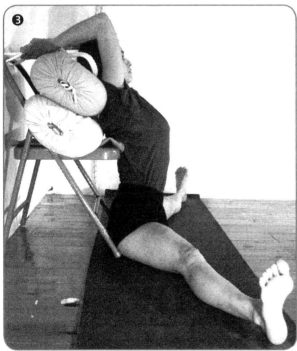

Variation 2: Holding the chair

Placing the chair in front helps to lift the chest and stabilize the pose.

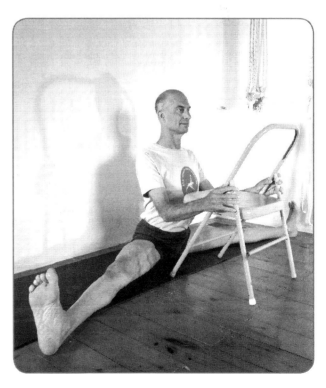

Dandasana

In this pose, the hands are used for lifting the chest. If needed, place two blocks under the palms.

 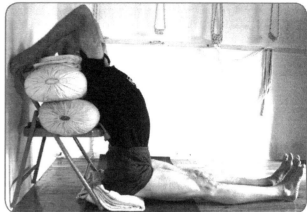

Virasana

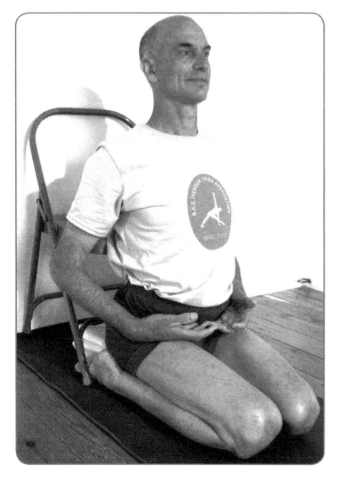 

Tadasana on the chair

It is possible to learn and practice the actions of the upper body in *Tadasana* when sitting on the chair. This is particularly suitable for people who cannot stand, but it can teach all students how to extend the spine, open the chest, and practice mindful breathing.

↻ Sit on the chair facing backwards with the legs inserted under the backrest. Keep the thighs parallel to the floor and the shins perpendicular forming 90^0 at the knees ❶. If you are tall, place a folded blanket on the seat, as in ❷; if the feet do not reach the floor, place suitable support under the feet (not shown).

↻ Stretch the arms down and catch the legs of the chair as low as possible. Work the arms and notice the effect on the shoulder blades and upper back.

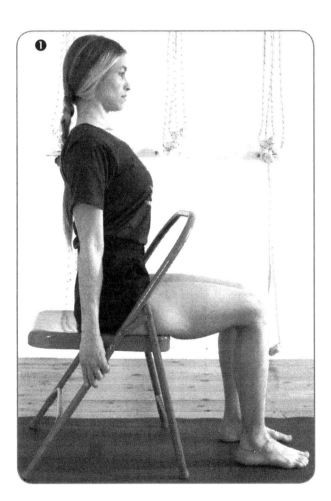
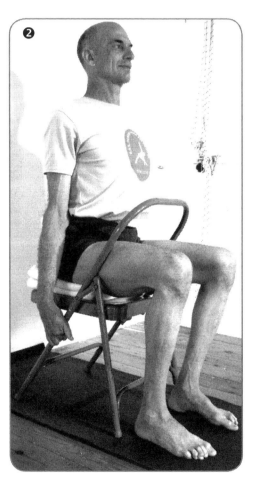

⮑ Now, interlock the fingers and stretch the arms upward as in *Urdhva Baddhanguliyasana* ❸.

⮑ Next, take the hands down and catch the backrest. Pull the chair to move the elbows and shoulders back and the chest forward.

⮑ This is a good way to practice *Pranayama*. Sitting on the chair makes it much easier to lift and stabilize the spine; furthermore, holding the backrest helps to open the chest. For deep breathing, always lower the head to the chest to perform *Jalandhara Bandha* ❹.

Working on *Tadasana* while sitting helps you focus on the upper body. Holding the chair makes the arms active and helps roll the shoulders back, move the shoulder blades in, and open the chest. Once learned, you can apply these same actions while standing in *Tadasana*.

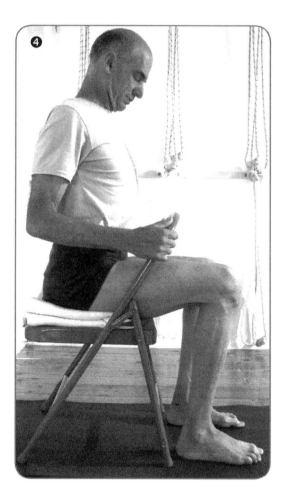

Chapter 3: Forward Extensions – Paschima Pratana Sthiti

Bending forward when sitting on the floor is difficult for many practitioners; it takes time to learn to extend the spine in a forward bend. Extending the spine is vital in these poses because it protects the inter-vertebra discs from being compressed, thus preventing injury.

In the following examples, the chair is used for learning how to extend the spine safely. We start with *Paschimottanasana* and then show some of the variations for other forward extensions.

Paschimottanasana

Variation 1: Sitting on the chair

➲ Place the chair on a sticky mat in front of the wall; put another folded sticky mat on its seat.

➲ Sit so that the buttock bones are near the edge of the seat and the feet are placed against the wall ❶. This way there is no danger of sliding off the chair. Another option is to secure the chair by placing its back against the wall, and place the feet against a block ❹.

➲ Put the palms on the seat and use them to lift the chest (this is *Dandasana* on chair) ❶.

➲ Raise the arms and stretch them up to get further extension of the spine and more lifting of the chest ❷.

↻ Move the chest forward, and while maintaining a concave back, move the hands backwards to hold the backrest behind you (if you cannot reach the backrest, loop a belt around it and hold it with both hands). Stay in this position to feel the lengthening of the front spine ❸.

↻ Now move the arms forward and catch the big toes while keeping the back concave. If the toes cannot be reached, loop a belt around the feet and hold it ❹.

↻ Bend forward and extend the upper body over the legs. You can take the arms backwards to hold the legs of the chair ❺.

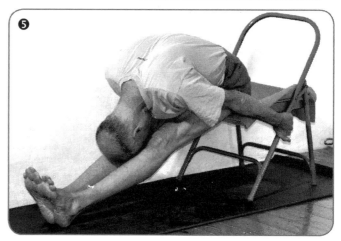

↻ Move the arms forward, hold the feet, and rest the forehead on the legs ❻.

↻ To relax more in the pose, place a folded blanket or a bolster on the legs to support the forehead ❼.

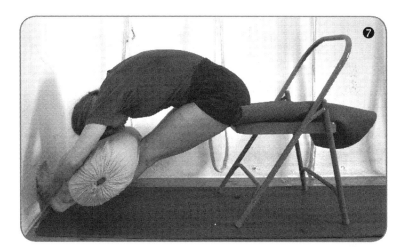

Most beginners find this variation very helpful. The downward slope of the legs eases the forward extension while gravity helps to release the spine.

Variation 2: In between two chairs

This is a more advanced variation which helps to open the back of the legs and increase the forward extension. It is suitable for advanced practitioners. The body is supported only on the buttock and heel bones. Pressing these four bones down helps to extend the trunk while keeping the inner organs soft.

- Sit on one chair and place another one at the appropriate distance (measured by the length of your legs). Put sticky-mats on both chairs.

- Hold the backrest of the chair you are sitting on and concave the back ❶.

- Lift the arms, extend upwards and then bend forward to hold the backrest of the other chair. Extend the arms in line with the sides of the trunk and pull the chair while pressing the heels down ❷. This will open and extend the sides of the body. Lifting the sides allows the spine to descend further toward the legs. If you cannot reach the backrest of the other chair, hold the seat or use a belt.

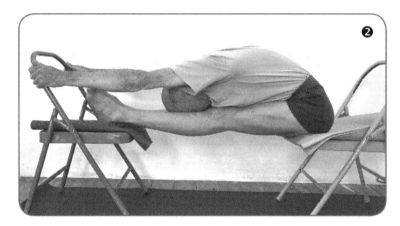

Variation 3: Resting the forehead on the chair

This variation helps less flexible people stay longer in the pose and enjoy quietness and relaxation. The cooling and relaxing effect of forward bends is not felt if the forehead is not rested on a support. This variation enables one to achieve the desired effect in case there is difficulty placing the forehead on one's legs.

- Sit on a folded blanket in front of the chair.
- Place the chair above the legs and push the toe mounds against the horizontal metal rung connecting the back legs of the chair. Make sure all the toe mounds are touching the chair equally (pay special attention to the big toe mound).
- Bend slightly forward and hold the backrest of the chair. Lift the chest and concave the back ❶.
- Bend forward to rest the forehead on the seat, keeping the arms in line with the sides of the body ❷.
- If the horizontal rung is too high for your feet, place the heels on a block ❸.

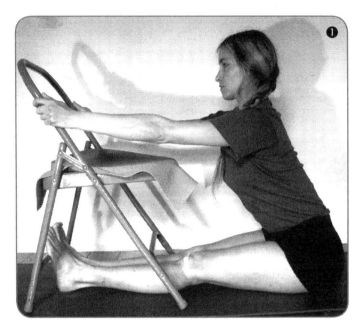

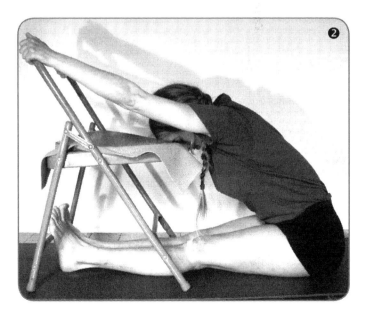

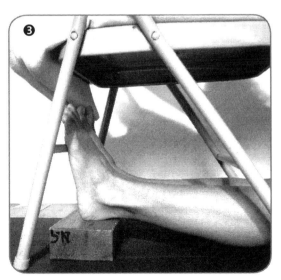

This variation helps one to open the feet and extend the legs. The legs become active without inducing tension in the upper body.

Variation 4: Pulling the legs of the chair

This variation is suitable for more advanced practitioners who wish to improve their forward extension. Compared with the previous variation, this one requires a more intense extension because the feet are supported against the **front** horizontal rung of the chair.

➲ Push the feet against the metal rung connecting the front legs of the chair and pull the chair with the arms. Lift up the sternum bone, concave the back and look upwards ❶.

➲ Now, lift the elbows and bend them sideways, extend the trunk forward and rest the head on the shins. ❷

Note that here the forehead is not supported on the seat but on the leg (if needed put a folded blanket on the shins).

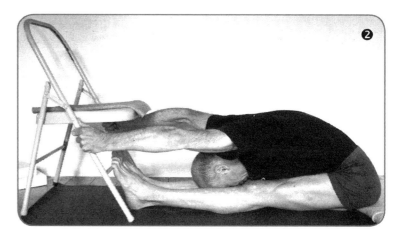

Variation 5: Chair inverted; pulling the seat

Here we invert the chair and use the bottom side of the seat to support the feet.

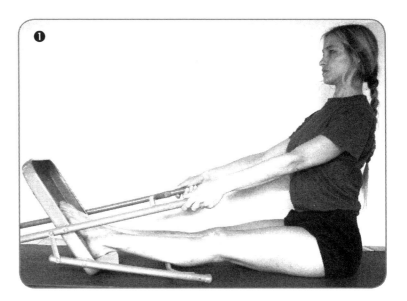

- Sit on a folded blanket and place a folded chair in front of you, with its legs towards you and its seat facing up.
- Unfold the chair slightly. Place the feet against the bottom of the seat. Hold the front legs of the chair and pull towards you. The heels are lifted slightly and placed on the bottom rim of the seat (place a sticky piece on it for cushioning).
- Lift the chest and concave the back ❶.
- Bend forward and grasp the sides of the seat. Adjust the arm by modifying the folding of the chair until you reach a comfortable distance.
- Place the upper arms on the front legs of the chair.
- Push the chair with your legs and pull it with your arms. Rest the forehead on the shins (place a folded blanket on the legs if needed) ❷.

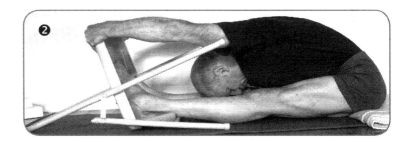

Using the chair in this way has several advantages:
1. The feet are fully pressed against the seat which provides a solid support for both the heels and the toe mounds.
2. The heels are slightly raised on the rim of the seat, helping to further open the back of the knees.
3. The legs of the chair support the arms and help to keep them lifted. This lift of the arms and elbows is important, since otherwise the sides of the body tend to close and shorten. When the elbows drop, the vertebras stick out and the back curves up (laterally), instead of being flat.

The next section shows a similar application of the chair for forward extensions in which one of the legs is bent.

The chair is used in two main ways:

- To support the forehead on the seat – this is helpful when one cannot extend the body to reach the straight leg, and
- For anchoring the hands – which helps to increase the forward traction. This is done by either holding the legs of the chair or inverting the chair upside down and holding the seat.

We have not attempted to present all the variations but instead have selectively shown how to apply some of the options.

Janu Sirsasana

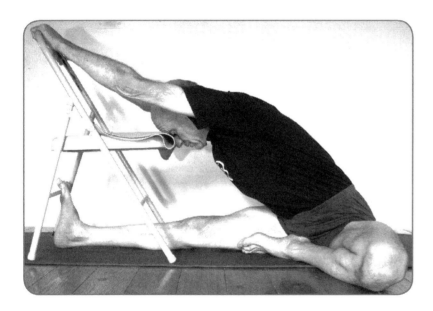

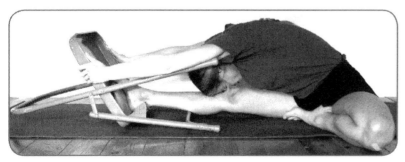

Triang Mukhaikapada Paschimottanasana

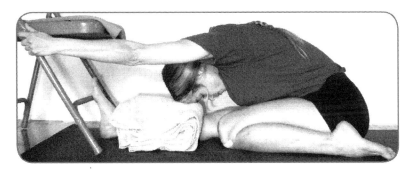

Ardha Padma Paschimottanasana

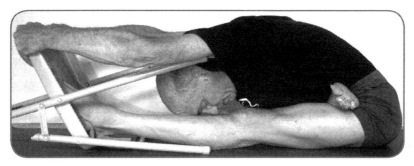

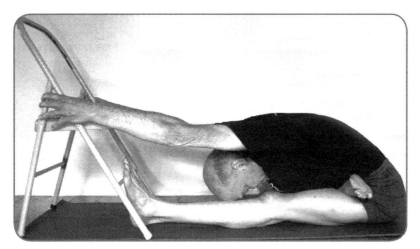

In *Ardha Padma Paschimottanasana*, the bent leg is held in place on the upper thigh of the straight leg; making it possible to sit on the chair to bend forward, very much like variation 1 of *Paschimottanasana* (see page 44).

Sitting on the chair gives a high support, thus creating more freedom to bend the leg into a half lotus position ❶, and to move the trunk forward ❷. The *Baddha* variation of the pose (catching the big toe of the bent leg) is shown in ❸.

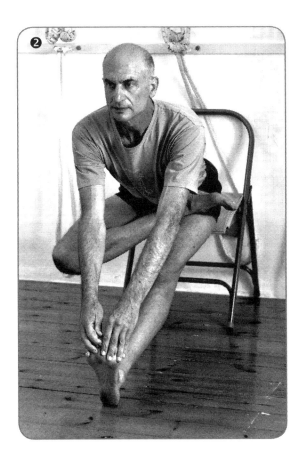

Marichyasana I

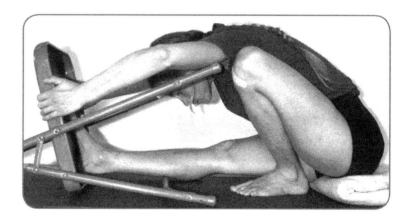

In the following two *asanas,* the chair is used to support the forehead. This variation helps people who have difficulty bending forward, to stay longer and to relax in the pose. In addition, the chair provides anchoring for the hands, helping the practitioner to extend the front side of the spine further forward.

Adho Mukha Baddha Konasana

Adho Mukha Upavistha Konasana

Urdhva Mukha Paschimottanasana I

Two ways of using the chair for this pose are presented.

Variation 1: Legs on the seat

- Sit on the floor and place the chair about 50 centimeters (20 inches) in front of you.
- Lift the legs and place the calf muscles on the edge of the seat.
- Extend the body upward and forward. Fold the upper body over the legs. Extend the arms forward and hold the backrest.

Variation 2: Sitting on the chair

- Place the chair with its back close to the wall. Sit on the chair facing its backrest.
- Lift the legs and place the calf muscles or the back of the knees on the backrest and and the feet on the wall.
- Extend the body upward and forward. Fold the upper body over the legs. Extend the arms forward and hold the feet.

Malasana

Two ways of using the chair for this pose are presented.

Variation 1: Sitting on the chair
- Sit on the chair facing the backrest.
- Lift the legs and place the back of the knees on the backrest.
- Lean forward and embrace the legs.

This variation is very relaxing. It can be used after practicing back bends, to relax the back and extend the regions of the spine that may have been compressed. It is also very soothing for the knees.

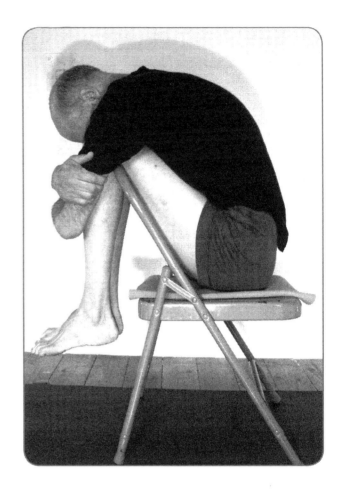

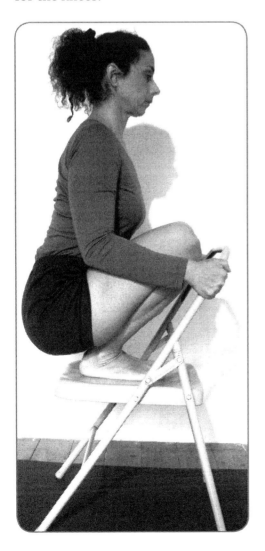

Variation 2: Standing on the chair
- Squat on the chair facing the backrest.
- To prevent falling back, hold the backrest.

When practicing this pose on the floor, one tends to roll backwards. One solution for this is to lift the heels on some support, but this will not extend the calf muscles. Using the chair in this way helps to move the shins forward while extending the calf muscles. This will improve the flexibility of the ankles.

Kurmasana

Kurmasana is a challenging forward bend which requires a lot of flexibility. With the help of the chair, everyone can enjoy it.

↪ Sit facing forward on the edge of the chair.

↪ Extend the body and the arms forward and place the palms on the floor away from your body **❶**.

↪ Gradually move the trunk in between the legs. Make the back convex and move the hands toward the back of the chair and hold its back legs **❷**.

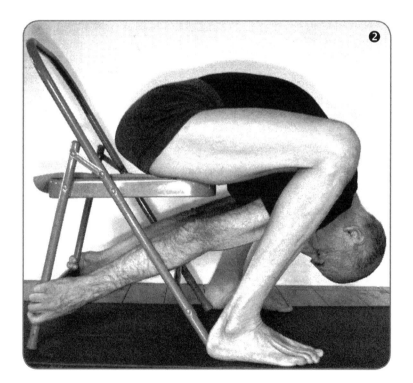

Pavana Muktasana

This variation of the pose, using two chairs, is very relaxing and provides deep rest for the abdominal organs and the lower back. It can be used to alleviate symptoms such as lower back pain, headache, and high blood pressure.

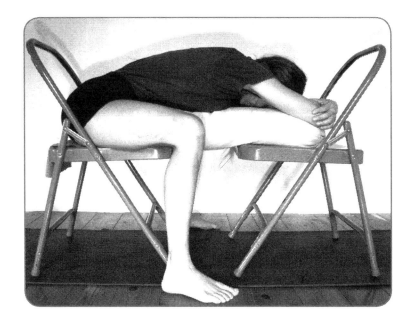

- ⮑ Place two chairs to face one another. Place a folded mat on one chair and a bolster on the other (lengthwise).
- ⮑ Sit on the mat and extend forward. Adjust the position of the other chair so that the abdomen and chest rest on the bolster.
- ⮑ You can fold the arms on the bolster as in ❶ or stretch them forward over the backrest, as in ❷.
- ⮑ If needed, use another bolster or a folded blanket to raise the support for the forehead.

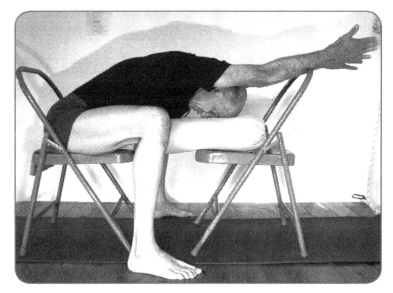

Parsva Pavana Muktasana

This is a variation of *Pavana Muktasana* with a side (*parsva*) stretch.

To stretch to the right side:

- Continuing from the previous pose, move the chair in front of you a little to the right.
- Turn the whole trunk from left to right and then lean on the bolster while extending forward.
- You can place the forehead or the left cheek on the bolster.

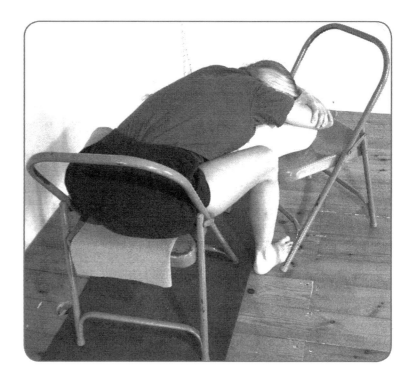

Chapter 4: Twists – Parivritta Sthiti

When twisting, the chair can be used in the following two ways:
- ⟳ Sitting on the chair – this helps to extend the spine from its root.
- ⟳ Sitting on the floor next to the chair and using it to increase the twisting action.

For some twisting *asanas* both ways are applicable.

Parsva Sukhasana

Variation 1: Sitting on the chair

To twist to the right side:
- ⟳ Place a sticky mat on the chair and a folded blanket on top. The sticky mat prevents the blanket from sliding.
- ⟳ Sit with crossed legs with the buttock bones on the blanket and the feet on the seat.
- ⟳ Turn to the right, roll the right shoulder back and hold the seat or the leg of the chair. The left hand holds the right knee.
- ⟳ Inhale and extend the spine, exhale and use the arms to twist.

The chair provides anchoring for the right hand, helping to increase the twist.

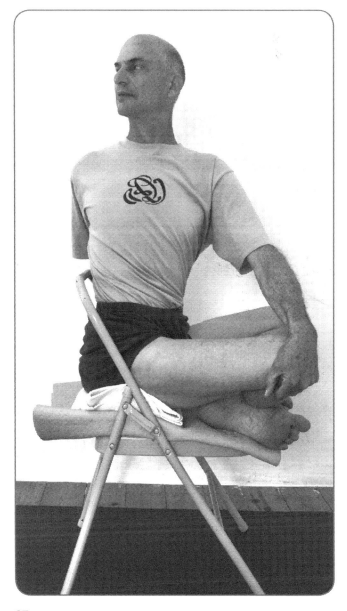

Variation 2: Sitting on the floor

In this variation, the chair is used when sitting on the floor.

To twist to the right side:

⮑ Sit with crossed legs on a folded blanket and place the chair in front and diagonally to your right.

⮑ Turn to the right. Place the left hand on the seat and the right hand on the wall (or on a block) behind you.

⮑ Use the chair support to extend the left side of the body and to lift the left armpit.

⮑ Inhale and extend the spine; exhale and use the arms to twist ❶.

⮑ Now, bend diagonally forward. Hold the backrest and lean the forehead on the seat (place a blanket or a bolster for cushioning) ❷.

The chair can also be placed behind you and used to support the right hand ❸.

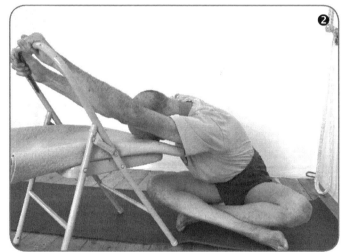

Bharadvajasana I on the Chair

Bharadvajasana I is a basic twisting pose. Twisting with a straight, extended spine is very beneficial for the back. Sitting on the chair enables one to extend the spine and twist along its axis. This popular variation helps to achieve the twisting action without compromising the spinal alignment. It can be used for releasing lower backache and is suitable for women during menstruation or pregnancy.

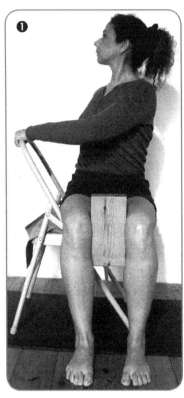

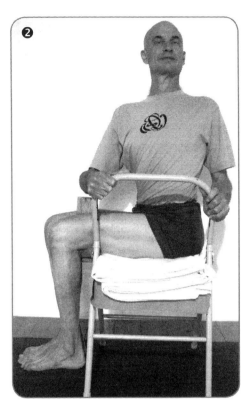

To twist to the right side:

⮑ Place a folded sticky mat on the seat. Sit sideways with the right side of the trunk facing the backrest ❶.

⮑ Make sure that the thighs are parallel to the floor, forming a 90^0 angle with the perpendicular shins. Tall practitioners may need to use a blanket or two to increase the height of the seat ❷, while short practitioners may need to place a support under their feet (not shown).

⮑ Keep the spine extended upward and twist to your right.

⮑ Hold the backrest. With each exhalation, increase the twist by using the left hand to pull and the right hand to push the backrest.

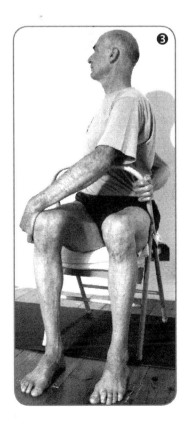

⮑ Keep both knees in line. A block held in between the thighs or knees can be used to stabilize them ❶.

⮑ To twist to the left, turn and sit with the left side facing the backrest ❷.

Another option is to sit facing the backrest. When twisting to the right:

- Insert the legs under the backrest and sit on the chair facing backwards.
- Twist to your right and place the right palm on the seat at the back. With the left hand, pull the outer right knee.
- Now, twist further and, if possible, grip the left side of the backrest with the right arm ❸. This helps to further rotate and open the right shoulder.

In this pose it is a challenge to keep the pelvis stabilized. If the pelvis moves, we get a turning action instead of a twist because the entire body turns. The sticky mat on the seat and the block between the legs help to stabilize the pelvis. The following is yet another good option to prevent the pelvis from sliding and turning:

- Insert the legs under the backrest and sit on the chair facing backwards.
- Depending on the width of the chair and your pelvis, place a wooden or foam block between the backrest and the right hip. The block should be held in place with slight pressure ❹.
- Turn to your right.

In addition to stabilizing the pelvis, the block creates compactness in the hip joints, helping to extend the spine and increase the twisting action.

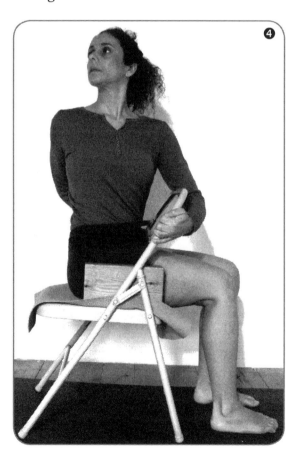

The following variation will provide immediate feedback on whether the pelvis has been turned.

⮑ Place the chair in front of the wall.

⮑ Insert the legs under the backrest and sit on the chair, knees facing the wall.

⮑ Place foam blocks (or other soft support) between the knees and the wall (maintain the right angle between the thighs and the shins).

⮑ Turn to the right and sense the pressure of the knees on the foam blocks. The right knee tends to lose contact; hence, extend the right thigh forward and keep the right knee pressing the block ❷.

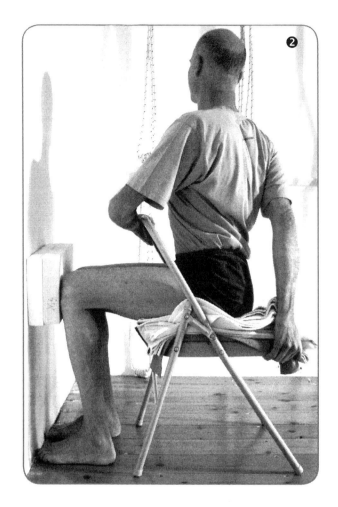

Bharadvajasana I (on the floor)

Here, *Bharadvajasana* is done as usual (sitting on the floor) and the chair is used to intensify the twisting action. To twist to the left:

- ➲ Sit in *Dandasana* and place the chair to your left.
- ➲ Fold the legs to the right, placing the right front ankle on the arch of to left foot.
- ➲ To prevent the body from tilting to the left, place a folded blanket under the left buttock.
- ➲ Twist to the left and hold the chair so that the right palm is higher than the left one.
- ➲ With each exhalation, use the right arm to pull the chair toward you and the left arm to push the chair. This will increase the twisting action.

When twisting, the side which is opposite to the twisting direction tends to drop and shorten. For example, when turning to the left, the right side tends to shorten and the spine tends to curve to the left. Using the chair helps to keep both sides of the trunk parallel.

Marichyasana III

When doing *Marichyasana III* on the floor it is difficult to lift the spine from its base. The following three examples show how the chair helps to achieve this lift.

Variation 1: Sitting on the chair

When practicing this *asana* on the floor a folded blanket is usually used to lift the buttocks. This enables the lift of the sacrum at the back and the pubic bone at the front in a parallel manner. However, a blanket is not always enough and one can benefit from sitting higher, on the chair.

To twist to the left:

- ➲ Place a support for the buttocks on the seat (two folded blankets or another similar support).
- ➲ Bend the left leg and place its heel on the seat.
- ➲ Twist to the left and place the right upper arm against the left outer knee. Hold the backrest with the left hand.

Observe how this variation helps to lift the trunk and separate the lower abdomen from the pelvis, enabling it to move more freely. The backrest provides an anchor for the back arm (left in the photo), helping to intensify the twist.

Variation 2: Sitting on the floor – chair on the side

To twist to the right:

⮩ Sit in *Dandasana* on a folded blanket and place the chair to your right.

⮩ Bend the right leg and place the heel close to the buttock bone.

⮩ Keeping the right leg pressed against the chair, twist to the right. Place the left elbow on the seat and hold the backrest. Place the right hand behind you and if needed, support it on a block ❶.

⮩ Another option is to hold the chair with both hands ❷.

The chair stabilizes the bent leg and provides an anchoring point for the opposite arm (left arm when twisting to the right).

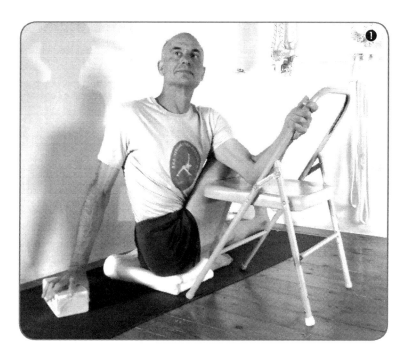

Variation 3: Sitting on the floor – chair behind

To twist to the right:

- ⮑ Sit in *Dandasana* on a folded blanket and place the chair behind you.
- ⮑ Bend the right leg and place the heel close to the buttock bone.
- ⮑ Twist to the right and place the right elbow on the seat. Press the left arm against the outer right knee, as usual.

Marichyasana I – Twist only

Marichyasana I is a forward bend, but the first stage of it is a twisting action. It is possible to practice this stage when sitting on the chair as shown in *Marichyasana III* (see page 68) but here we only show the variation on the floor, next to the chair.

To twist to the left:

⮑ Sit in *Dandasana* on a folded blanket and place the chair to your left.

⮑ Bend the right leg and place the heel close to the buttock bone.

⮑ Twist to the left and hold the seat with the right arm. The left hand can be placed on a block, or used to push the chair.

This variation can be practiced safely by women during menstruation as a substitute for *Marichyasana III*.

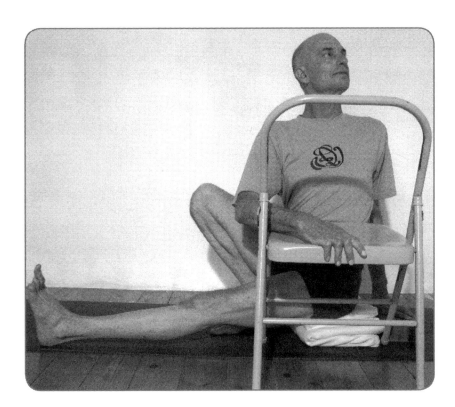

Ardha Matsyendrasana I

The special cross of the legs in this *asana* is challenging. The chair is used to stabilize the pose and increase the twisting action.

To twist to the right:

↪ Sit in *Dandasana* and place the chair to your right.

↪ Bend the left leg and sit on the inner arch of the foot. Place a folded blanket between the foot and the buttock in order to raise the seat.

↪ Bend the right leg and cross it over the left thigh. The right ankle should firmly touch the outer left knee. In order to keep the right shin perpendicular, place a foam block between the outer knee and the seat.

↪ Twist to the right and hold the seat with the left hand. You can support the right hand against the wall or on a block ❶.

The chair makes the left arm more effective in lifting the left side of the body and provides support to the right leg, thus enabling one to increase the twisting action.

One can also hold the chair with both hands for a left twist ❷.

Another option is to place the chair behind you to support the right hand ❸.

Ardha Matsyendrasana II

This is an advanced variation of *Ardha Matsyendrasana I* (LOY, Pl. 330-1). It provides a greater lateral twist to the spine.

With the right leg bent (twisting to the left):

⊃ Put a folded sticky mat on the chair and sit on it.

⊃ Bend the right leg to *Ardha Padmasana* (half lotus), then twist to your left and hold the backrest with the left hand. Grip the seat on the left side with the right hand ❶.

⊃ Now bend forward and swing the left arm behind the back. With the left hand grasp the right ankle or shin ❷.

Sitting on the chair the same way, you can also twist to the right:

⊃ With your right arm hold the backrest and turn to the right.

⊃ From there swing the right arm back to catch the right foot ❸.

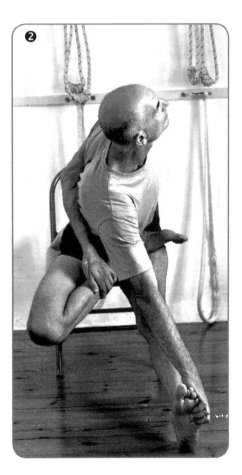

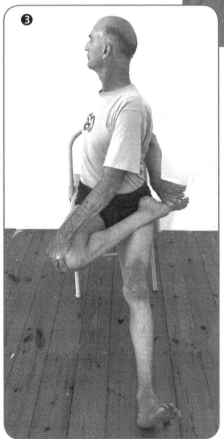

Pashasana

Pashasana is an advanced twist (LOY Pl. 328 & 329). The chair can be used to prepare the body for the final pose.

Variation 1: Sitting on the chair - feet on the floor

This is an easy way to learn the twisting action. To twist to the left:

- ➲ Sit on the chair with legs together. Bend slightly forward and twist to the left.
- ➲ Place the right elbow against the left outer knee and grip the backrest with the left hand.
- ➲ Use the arms and the exhalations to gradually increase the twist ❶.
- ➲ Then, slide the right arm down to grip the leg of the chair.
- ➲ Concave the right side of the back, roll the left shoulder back and twist further to the left ❷.

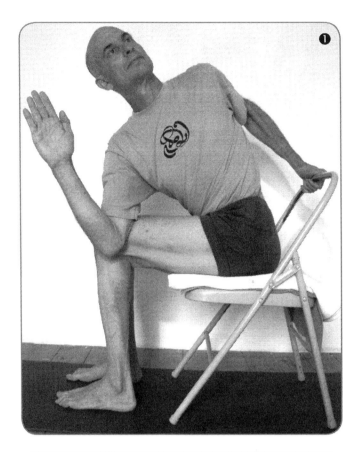

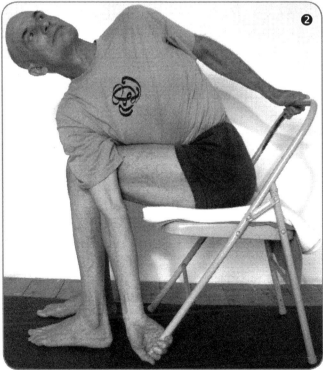

Variation 2: Sitting on the chair - legs on the backrest

To twist to the left:

⮕ Sit on the chair facing backwards and place the back of the knees on the backrest.

⮕ Twist to the left, placing the right elbow against the left outer knee and the left hand on the seat.

Here, the seat provides the fulcrum for the twist, while the legs are held in position by the backrest. The support of the backrest is very soothing for the knees.

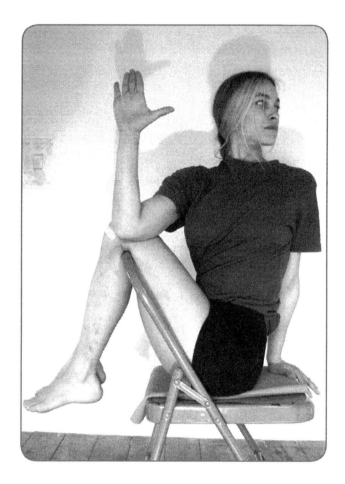

Variation 3: Squatting - chair behind

This variation better resembles the final pose which is done in a squatting position.

To twist to the left:

- ⮌ Stand in front of the chair and bend the knees gradually, while twisting to the left.
- ⮌ Place the left hand on the seat and push down to help move the knees forward.
- ⮌ Move the right elbow across the left leg and push it against the outer knee ❶.
- ⮌ Now bend further into a squatting position ❷.

Many people tend to fall back when practicing this pose. Supporting the back hand on the chair prevents this. It helps to move the knees forward and extend the calf muscles.

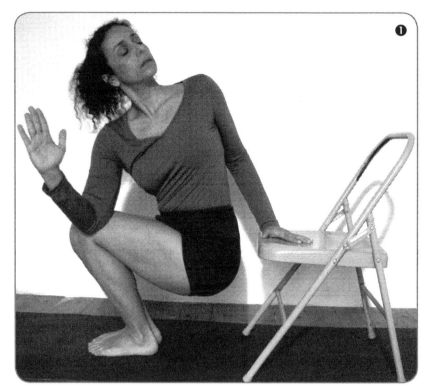

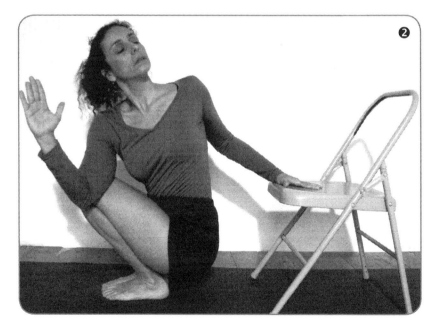

Variation 4: Squatting - chair on the side

This variation is closest to the final pose.

To twist to the right:

⤳ Stand and place the chair to your right.

⤳ Bend the knees while twisting to the right and hold the chair with both hands.

⤳ Cross the left upper arm over the right knee. Place the elbow on the seat and grasp the backrest ❸.

⤳ With each exhalation, use your arms to twist the trunk further.

⤳ If you tend to fall backwards, place a folded blanket under the heels.

The chair support helps to intensify the twist.

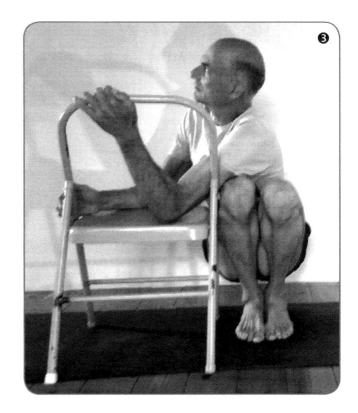

Utthita Marichyasana III

This variation of *Marichyasana III* is done while standing (hence, the name *Utthita*). The standing posture helps to extend the spine. Therefore, this is one of the best poses for releasing the lower back and creating movement between the vertebras.

To twist to the right:

- ◌ Place the chair near the wall and increase the height of the seat, so that when putting your foot on it, the knee is higher than the hip.
- ◌ Stand with your right side touching the wall and the chair in front of you.
- ◌ Lift the right leg and place the foot on the support.
- ◌ Twist to the right and place the left hand against the outer right knee.
- ◌ Use the right hand to push the wall and the left hand to pull the right outer knee ❶.
- ◌ Press the right hip to the wall and do not allow the left thigh to move forward.
- ◌ Inhale and extend upward; exhale and twist.

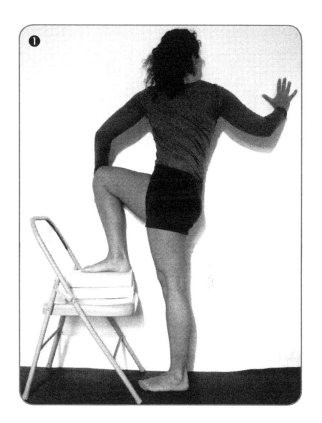

When twisting to the left ❷ the right (standing) thigh tends to move forward. A helper can stabilize it and increase the twist. The helper pushes the practitioner's hips to the wall and supports his right (standing) leg to prevent it from moving forward.

At the same time, the helper can roll the left shoulder backwards and push his/her right side ribs to the right and toward the wall.

The helper should not apply force directly on the shoulder but rather place his/her left hand in between the practitioner's shoulder and chest and be careful not to pull too strongly.

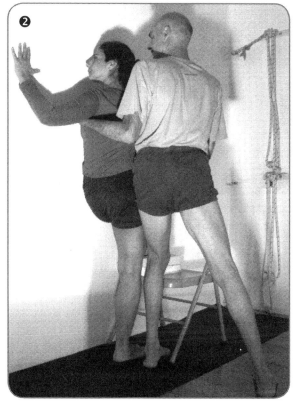

Chapter 5: Inversions - Viparita Sthiti

Salamba Sirsasana

Variation 1: Sirsasana on two chairs

This variation enables you to benefit from the tremendous positive effects of Sirsasana, "the king of all asanas", even when you cannot do the pose independently because of reasons such as:

- Difficulty in lifting the shoulders and creating enough length in the neck,
- Pain or sensitivity in the neck,
- Injury to the skull.

To enter the pose:

- Place two chairs facing each other next to the wall. Roll two sticky mats so that they have equal in diameter and density and place one on each seat. The distance between the chairs should allow the head to enter in between the seats.
- Stand in front of the chairs. Bend forward, move the head down in between the two chairs and rest the shoulders on the rolled sticky mats.
- Now, gently draw the chairs closer to each other, and to the neck. The rolled sticky mats should support the flesh between the neck and the two shoulders symmetrically.
- Place the back of the shoulders against the wall ❶.
- Place the palms on the chairs and lift the legs.
- Place the heels against the wall and stay in the pose.
- Make sure the heels and the back of the head are in line. Keep lifting yourself by pushing the shoulders into the chairs ❷.

Variation 2: Using the chair to support the shoulder blades

↪ Place a chair with its back against the wall.

↪ To prevent the chair from folding, you may place a 10 Kg (20 pounds) weight on the seat (not shown).

↪ Depending on your size and the chair's height, you may need to raise the surface slightly. In that case, place two or three folded blankets on the sticky mat and possibly another lengthwise three-folded blanket to support the head ❶.

↪ Place the crown of the head on the mat or the folded blanket, just below the front edge of the seat. Straighten the legs and move forward to touch the seat with your shoulder blades.

↪ Go up to *Sirsasana* lifting one leg after the other ❷ ❸. If you find it difficult to lift the legs, ask a friend to help you.

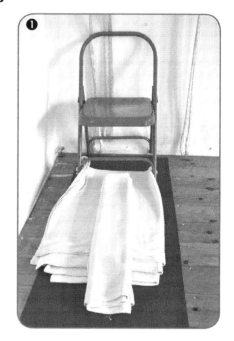

Note:

In order to protect the head and neck from excessive pressure in *Sirsasana* it is crucial to lift the shoulder girdle and to take the shoulder blades deep into the body. In this variation, the chair helps the arm and shoulder muscles to hold the shoulder blades in place. Study how strongly these muscles should work in free-standing *Sirsasana*.

The chair blocks the movement of the shoulders backward as one lifts the legs, thus makes it more challenging then usual. If you find it too difficult, ask a friend to help you.

Sirsasana Variations

The following variations in *Sirsasana* can be practiced using the chair as the support for one or both legs.

Eka Pada Sirsasana

Urdhva Dandasana

Parsvaika Pada Sirsasana

Pindasana in Sirsasana

This advanced variation in *Sirsasana* is possible if you can interlock your legs to *Padmasana* (the Lotus) while standing on the head (possibly with the back against the wall). In the final pose, the legs are lowered until the shins touch the upper arms (LOY, Pl. 218). The chair provides a higher support and therefore enables a longer, less stressful duration ❶❷.

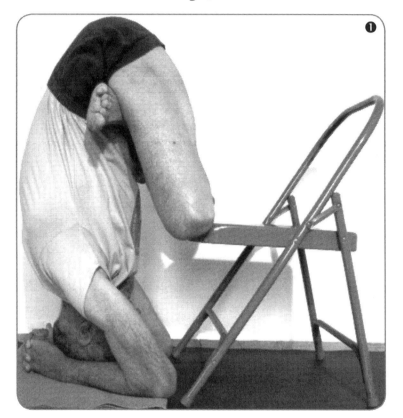

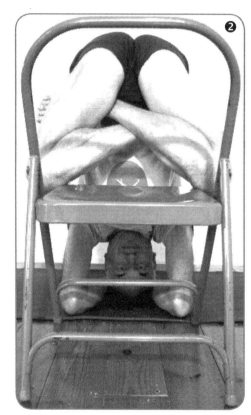

Place a bolster on the chair for a higher and softer support ❸.

Sirsasana Viparita Karani

The common variation of *Viparita Karani* is practiced with the shoulders and back of the neck resting on the floor. However, this *Sirsasana* variation of the pose is practiced with the crown of the head resting on the floor.

Note: This is an advanced variation – do not try it without proper guidance.

To get into the pose:

⮂ Place the chair near the wall, and a folded blanket slightly away from the chair. The height of the blanket depends on your height and the chair's height.

⮂ Sit sideways on the chair and roll to place the legs on the wall. Insert the arms in between the legs of the chair.

⮂ Slowly slide down from the chair, arch the back, and keep sliding until the top of the head rests on the blanket.

⮂ Stretch the legs vertically up and stay in the pose ❶.

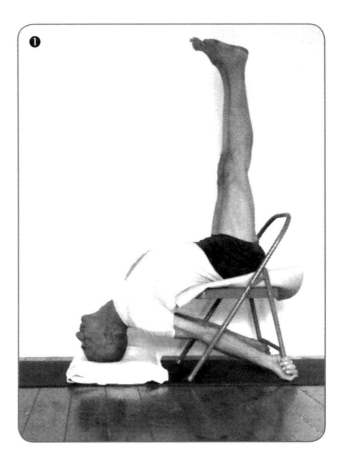

From this pose it is possible to move directly to *Salamba Sirsasana* as shown in ❷ to ❺.

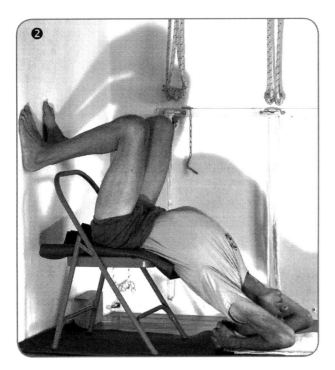

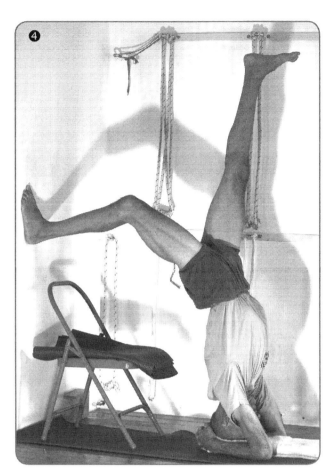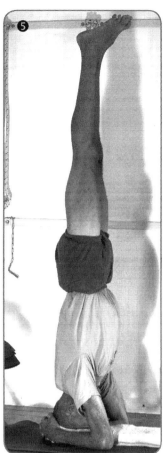

It is a nice way to enter *Sirsasana* since the chair helps to extend the neck and spine and to open the chest. This can be maintained when moving to *Sirsasana*. However, one should be very experienced and stable in *Sirsasana* before attempting it.

Pincha Mayurasana

Pincha Mayurasana (LOY, Pl. 357) requires balance, strength and mobility of the shoulders.
You can start by using the chair to prepare the shoulders for the pose.
<u>Note</u>: This variation requires a great deal of movement in the shoulders. Beginners may skip it.

↻ Lie with the upper back on the chair and insert the head and arms under the backrest ❶. If you have long upper arms, use a blanket or two to raise the seat until the distance between the rung and the seat matches the length of the upper arms.

↻ Bend your elbows to catch the back rung or the back legs. The hands and elbows should be shoulder width apart ❶.

↻ If your palms do not reach the rung ask your teacher to help you or try to use the right hand to help the left to catch, and vice versa. After a few times, you may be able to catch with both hands. Another option is to loop a belt around the rung and catch the belt.

↻ Slide back to the chair until the head is supported on the seat, and the elbows are just above the palms.

↻ Lift the pelvis; you may straighten the legs, but keep lifting the buttocks ❷.

↻ Roll the elbows from outside in, to maintain them shoulder width apart.

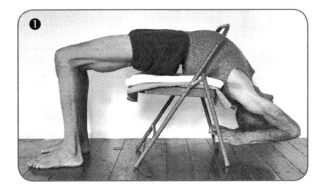 

This variation opens the shoulders and prepares for *Pincha Mayurasana* in which there should be a 90⁰ angle between the lower and the upper arms.

In many cases, the shoulder blades stick out, the front ribs push forward and the buttocks drop back. The following variation can be used to support the shoulder blades, keep the pose vertical and reduce load on the lower back. Practicing this way will help you to open the chest and increase movement in the shoulder region.

To use the chair:

- Place the chair next to the wall, with the seat facing you.
- Place the forearms on the floor, under the chair. The elbows should be shoulder width apart and the forearms parallel to each other. If you cannot maintain the proper width, place a block between the palms and tighten a belt around the elbows.
- Raise the buttocks and support the shoulder blades against the front edge of the chair.
- Lift the legs to *Pincha Mayurasana*. Stretch the whole body up and stay in the pose ❶.

You can hang a belt on the seat to prevent the chair from folding and to ensure that the elbows will remain under the shoulders and will not slide outward.

- Hang a belt on the seat ❷.
- Insert the arms inside the loop, and place the elbows at shoulder width. The belt should be adjusted so that it will embrace the elbows and the seat with slight pressure.
- Lift into *Pincha Mayurasana* ❸.

A helper sitting on the chair can gently lift and pull your lower front ribs as in ❹. The chair keeps the shoulder blades tucked in and prevents the shoulders from shrinking toward the floor, thus helping the upward extension.

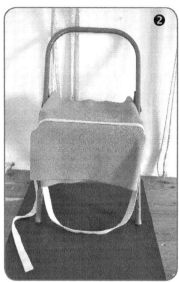

Salamba Sarvangasana I

This is one of the poses in which the chair is often used and is commonly called *"Chair Sarvangasana"*. The chair support enables deep relaxation and makes the pose restorative for the body and mind. It helps to open the chest and improve breathing in the upper chest region. The chair stabilizes the pose to the extent that even people suffering from neck problems or tightness in the shoulders can do it safely.

To use the chair:
- Place the chair next to the wall, with its backrest 10-15 centimeters (4-6 inches) from the wall.
- Put a folded blanket on top of a sticky mat on the seat.
- Spread a blanket under the chair and place a bolster on the floor parallel to the front of the chair.
- Sit sideways on the chair then roll to move the legs toward the wall. While holding the backrest, place the heels in the space between the backrest and the wall and pull yourself toward the wall until the buttocks are close to the wall ❶.
- Now you are lying safely balanced on the chair, so you can release the backrest, move the arms under the seat, insert them in between the front legs of the chair and grip the back legs ❷.

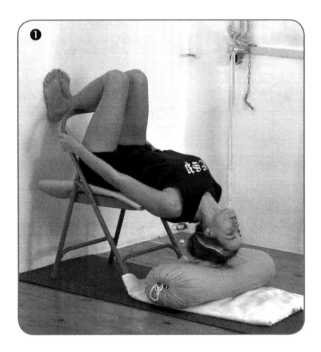
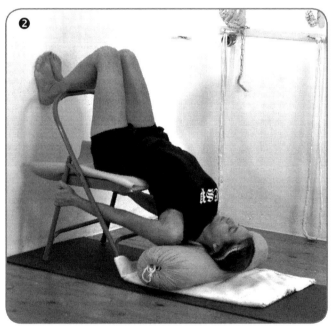

- Slowly slide down and rest the shoulders on the centerline of the bolster. Use the arms to pull the shoulders back until the back of the neck rests freely on the rounded edge of the bolster. Your weight should be distributed between the chair and the bolster.

⟳   Hold the back horizontal rung of the chair with the palms facing up.

⟳   The legs can lean against the wall ❸ or stretch vertically upward ❹.

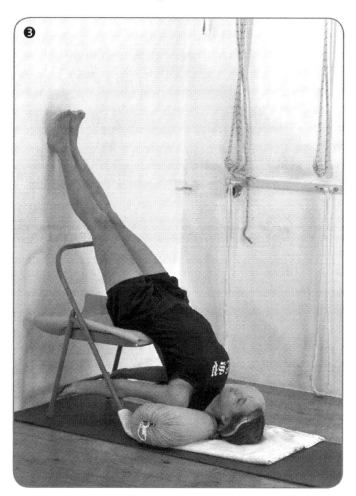

Notes:

1. Using the wall is optional; the pose can also be practiced without the wall.
2. If the neck feels compressed or if the seat is too high for you, place a triple-folded blanket under the bolster to raise the shoulders from the floor (not shown).
3. If the seat feels too low, place another folded blanket on the seat to support the sacrum ❹.

Variations of Chair Sarvangasana

The legs can be placed in *Baddha Konasana*, with the feet supported on the backrest.

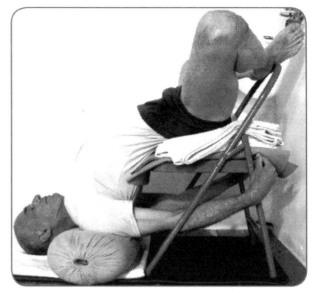

In some cases, it is more convenient to loop a belt around the backrest to provide a lower support for the feet.

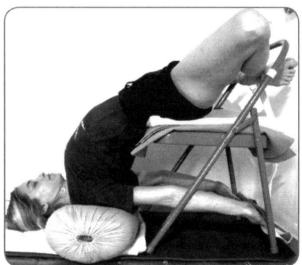

The legs can also be in *Padmasana*.

These leg variations give more lift to the back and a further opening of the chest.

Bending the elbows around the front legs of the chair intensifies the opening of the chest.

From there you can move to *Pindasana* in *Sarvangasana*.

Halasana & Variations (back against the chair)

To go to *Halasana*:

⮑ From *Chair Sarvangasana*, lower the legs to the floor and move to *Halasana*. Stretch the legs and place the top of the toes on the floor (if you find it hard to reach the floor, place a low stool beneath the toes).

⮑ Keep holding the chair.

⮑ Now, pull the chair toward you to support your back with the front edge of the seat. If possible, bend the elbows around the front legs of the chair ❶.

⮑ Now, lift yourself back into *Sarvangasana*. This time the body should be vertical as in the classic pose ❷.

⮑ Lower one leg to the floor for *Eka Pada Sarvangasana* (LOY, Pl. 250) ❸. Then change, and lower the other leg.

⮑ Lower one leg to the side for *Parsvaika Pada Sarvangasana* (LOY, Pl. 251) ❹. Then change, and lower the other leg.

⮑ Then go back to *Halasana* and practice variations such as *Karnapidasana*, *Supta Konasana*, *Pindasana* in *Sarvangasana* (LOY, Pl. 269), *Parsva Halasana* and more (only *Parsva Halasana* is shown here ❺).

Ardha Halasana & Variations (feet on the chair)

Full *Halasana* is practiced with toes on the floor. This variation of the pose, with toes on the seat, is called *Ardha* (half) *Halasana*.

To enter the pose:

- Stack 4 to 6 folded blankets to form a raised platform for the arms and shoulders.
- Place the chair at the appropriate distance from the edge of the blankets, on the side where the head will be.
- Lie with the back on the platform so that the shoulders are set about 5 centimeters (2 inches) in from the edge and the head is on the floor (it is recommended to place an additional blanket under the platform as a cushion for the head).
- Lift the hips and roll back until the tips of the toes reach the chair behind the head.
- Stretch your arms behind your back, interlock the fingers and press the elbows down toward the floor. Stretch the legs, lift the front thighs, and tighten the knees ❶.
- After several minutes in *Ardha Halasana* lift the right leg up ❷ then change, and lift the other leg.
- Finally, you can lift both legs (one after the other) into *Sarvangasana*.

⮑ From there, draw the chair further toward you, bend the legs, and use the chair for *(Ardha) Karnapidasana* ❸ ❹.

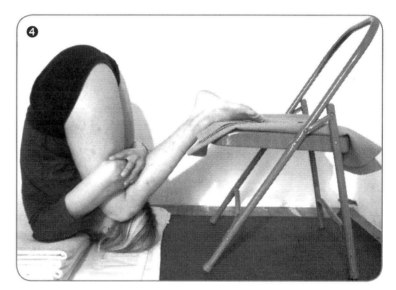

⮑ If you can place the legs in *Padmasana* (the Lotus), then use the chair to do *Pindasana* in *Sarvangasana* ❺.

⮂ You can place two chairs at both sides diagonally from the platform, to support the leg that moves down in *Parsvaika Pada Sarvangasana* ❶.

⮂ Then lower both legs to the chairs to *(Ardha) Supta Konasana* ❷.

Ardha Halasana is a recommended way to learn *Sarvangasana*. Many beginners find it difficult to lift the upper back and place themselves on the heads (tops) of the shoulders. In *Ardha Halasana* the high support of the feet enables one to achieve this lift with more ease.

<u>Note</u>: This pose can also be performed passively, without the strong arm and leg stretch, as a way to extend and relax the back (see Restorative *Ardha Halasana* on page 98).

Niralamba Sarvangasana

Chair Sarvangasana has been shown before with the back facing the wall but it can also be done with the front facing the wall. It can be used as a preparation for *Niralamba* (with no support) *Sarvangasana* because you can balance with only the finger and the tips of the toes pressed against the wall (instead of using the arms to support the back).

To enter the pose from the chair:

↪ Place the chair facing the wall, about half a meter (20 inches) away from the wall.

↪ Spread a blanket between the chair and the wall and put a bolster on it. Allow enough space between the bolster and the wall for the head and neck to fit in.

↪ Sit on the chair and slide down into the pose as explained in the instructions for *"Chair Sarvangasana"* (see page 85).

↪ Lift the body off the chair, stretch it up and place the toes against the wall.

↪ Move the arms toward the wall and place the finger tips against it. Support yourself in this way and stay in the pose (this is *Niralamba Sarvangasana I.* LOY Pl. 236) ❶.

↪ Then, stretch the arms along the sides of the body (this is *Niralamba Sarvangasana II.* LOY, Pl. 237) ❷.

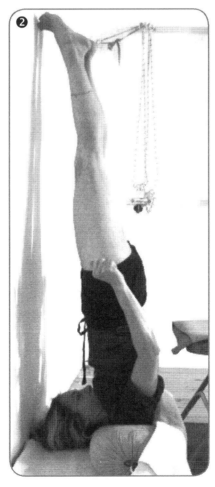

From there you can use the chair and the wall to perform *Karnapidasana* and *Supta Konasana* as follows:

- ⮥ Move the arms back, insert them under the chair, and grip its back legs.

- ⮥ Bend the knees and place the shins and feet against the wall ❸.

- ⮥ From there, spread the legs wide apart to *Supta Konasana* and roll the buttocks toward the wall (❹ ❺),

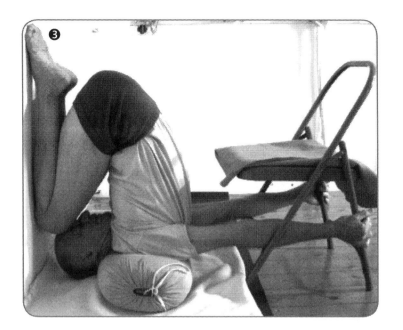

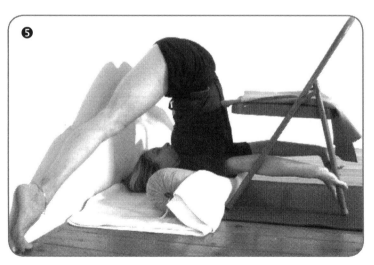

Wall Halasana and Sarvangasana

Halasana and *Salamba Sarvangasana* can be practiced with the back leaning against the wall. This is another restorative and very relaxing way to do these poses. It is possible but rather difficult to roll into the pose from the floor. The chair makes it easier to enter the pose and is used later to support the legs for *Halasana* and its variations.

To enter the pose from the chair:
- Place the chair facing the wall about half a meter (20 inches) away from the wall.
- Place a blanket between the chair and the wall and put a bolster on it. The bolster should touch the wall. Sometimes a bolster will not suffice; in this case, put another triple-folded blanket under the bolster.
- Kneel on the chair and place the palms on the bolster ❶.
- Slowly lower yourself toward the floor, controlling the movement with your arms ❷.
- Roll the head in and rest your shoulders on the bolster. Move the shoulders back toward the wall and then lean the back against the wall. Put the legs on the chair. This is *Ardha Halasana* ❸.

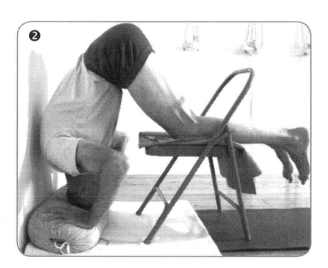

➲ After several minutes, move on to *Sarvangasana*. Here, the whole back of the body rests on the wall ❹.

➲ You can support the pelvis by placing a foam block between the wall and the pelvis ❺.

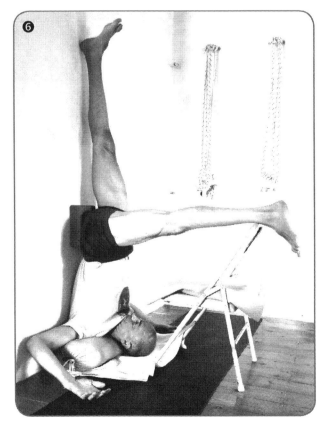

➲ From there you can practice some variations like *Eka Pada Sarvangasana* ❻,

➲ And *Karnapidasana* ❼.

Restorative Ardha Halasana

The chair or a bench can support the thighs in *Ardha Halasana*. This is a very relaxing pose. It calms the brain and helps to reduce stress. It is also helpful to alleviate lower back problems.

↻ Place the chair and spread a blanket next to its side. Place two bolsters in a T shape: one bolster to support the shoulders and the other to help with the "take-off" (entering the pose) and "landing" (exiting the pose). Place one or two folded blankets on the seat ❶.

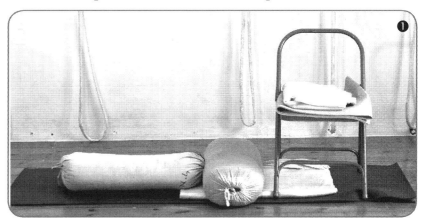

The reason for using the side of the chair is that otherwise, the horizontal rung will not let the head move underneath the chair (If the chair has no rungs, you can place its front against the shoulder-supporting bolster).

↻ Lie with the shoulders on the supporting bolster, the back on the vertical bolster and the head under the chair ❷.

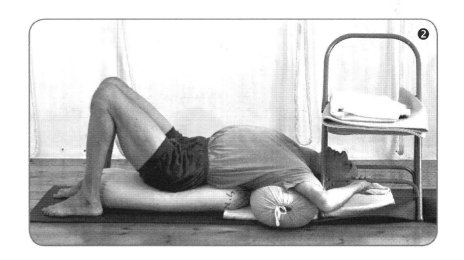

↻ Roll yourself up and place the legs on the support of the chair.

↻ Stretch the arms back. Interlock the fingers and move the shoulders back until they rest on the center line of the bolster.

↻ Now release the arms to the sides and relax in the pose ❸.

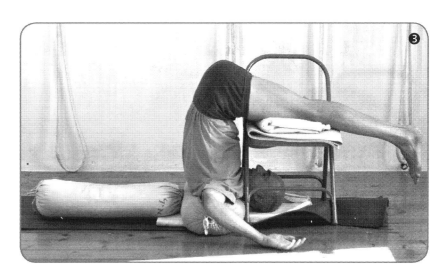

Setu Bandha Sarvangasana

This pose is part of the *Sarvangasana* cycle. Advanced practitioners enter into it by arching back from *Salmba Sarvangasana*. The chair can be used to learn this action. The chair is used to provide higher support for the legs, so one can drop half way instead of dropping all the way to the floor.
To use the support of the chair:

- Prepare a supporting platform for *Sarvangasana* as explained in the section "*Ardha Halasana* & Variations (feet on chair)" (see page 91).

- Place the chair at the appropriate distance from the platform on the side to which your back will face. You can place the chair next to the wall but this is not mandatory.

- Perform *Salmba Sarvangasana*, then arch back, bend the knees, and place them one by one on the chair ❶.
Straighten the legs. If the chair is next to the wall, push the feet against the wall. This will increase the arch and the opening of the chest ❷.

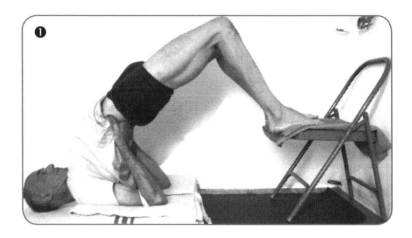

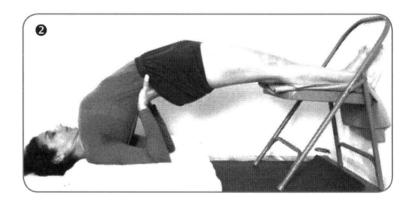

From here you can continue on to some other interesting variations such as:

Lift one leg at a time to *Eka Pada Setu Bandha Sarvangasana* (LOY Pl. 260) ❸.

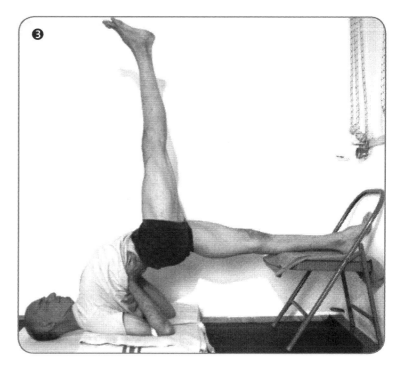

Or, bring the legs to *Padmasana* and place them on the chair for *Uttana Padma Mayurasana* ❹ (Remember that in the final pose the knees should descend all the way to the floor , see LOY Pl. 267).

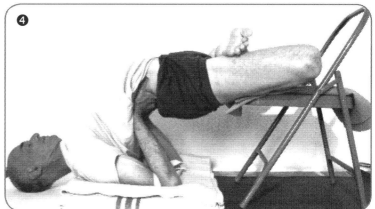

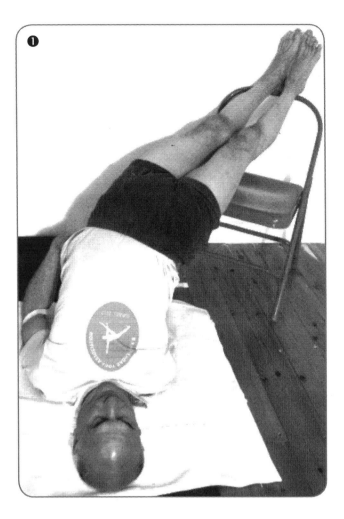

The chair can also be placed diagonally to the side in order to use the backrest as a support for *Parsva Sarvangasana* (LOY Pl. 254) ❶ ❷ and *Parsvaika Pada Setu Bandha Sarvangasana* ❸. You will need two chairs (or someone to move the chair from side to side).

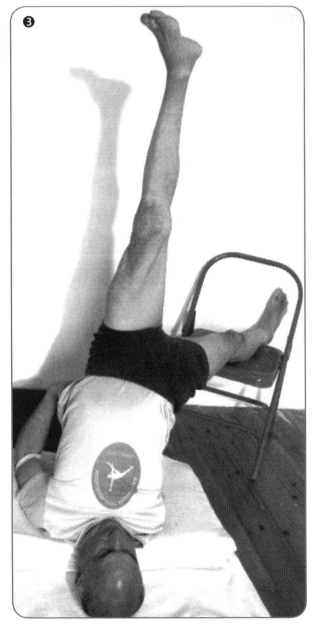

Chapter 6: Backward Extensions – Purva Pratana Sthiti

The chair offers many options for opening the chest, elongating the lower back and working the back muscles in preparation for independent back arching.

Salabhasana

You can use the chair to learn the chest action of *salabahasana*. Support the palms on the seat and press down to lift the chest while arching the upper back.

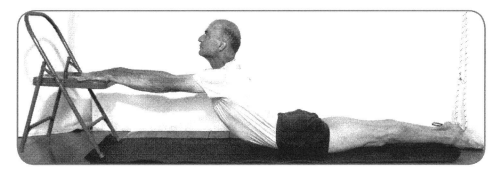

This variation of *Salabahasana*, in which the arms are stretched forward and the palms are supported, is especially useful for people who suffer from lower back pain. It enables a good workout for the back muscles with only moderate load on the lumbar spine.

Urdhava Mukha Svanasana

In this pose, the arms are used for lifting and opening the chest. For many people the arms feel too short for this action. This is where the chair can help.

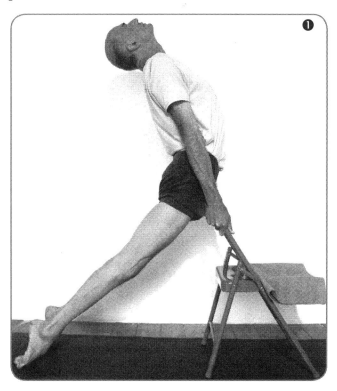

Variation 1: Hands on the backrest
- ↻ Place the chair in front of you with the backrest facing you.
- ↻ Hold the backrest and move the pelvis forward until the front groins touch the backrest.
- ↻ Now, arch the back. Roll the shoulders back and down. Extend the spine and neck and look up ❶. Move the tail bone in. Tighten the knees. Lift and open the chest.

Compared with the classic pose, the load on the arms is decreased, making it easier to lift the chest and concentrate on the leg action.

Variation 2: Hands on the seat

⮑ Place the chair in front the of you with the seat facing you. Place the palms on the seat. Move the pelvis forward until the front groins touch the seat. Arch the back. Roll the shoulders back and down. Extend the spine and neck and look up.

⮑ To help roll the shoulders back, you can turn the palms out ❷.

The chest should move forward in between the arms. If the seat is narrower than your chest, place a wooden plank on the seat and position the palms on its ends. (Put a piece of sticky mat under the plank to prevent it from sliding) ❸.

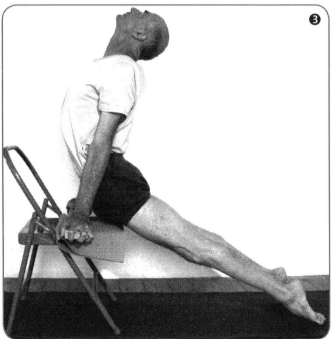

Dwi Pada Viparita Dandasana

When done independently this is an advanced back arch (LOY, Pl. 516) but with the chair almost everybody can stay in the pose and enjoy its benefits. Following, are several ways of using the chair for this purpose.

Variation 1: Legs inserted under the backrest

This is the classic preparation for the actual pose. It requires a belt and a sticky mat. Most people require some adjustment of the seat height (using a folded blanket) and/or heel support (using blocks).

Note: Your pelvis needs to fit through the seat and the backrest; for this reason, the metal back plate that is usually part of the original chair must be removed.

To do the pose follow these instructions:

⊃ Place the chair with its backrest toward the wall at the appropriate distance, so that while sitting the heels will reach the wall. Put a folded sticky mat on the seat and possibly a folded blanket for cushioning.

⊃ Sit with the thighs under the backrest, facing the wall. Tighten a belt around the upper thighs.

⊃ Holding the backrest, lie back on the seat so that the shoulder blades are aligned with the front edge of the seat.

⊃ Lift and open the chest. Use the arms to activate the shoulder blades ❶.

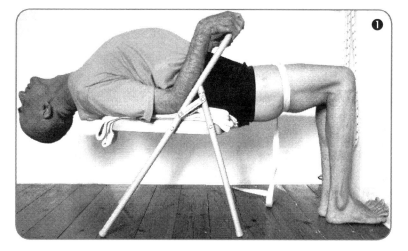

⊃ Stay in this position for a while, then slide further down toward the floor, until the bottoms of the shoulder blades just pass the front edge of the seat. Insert the arms in between the front legs of the chair and grip the back rung (palms facing up) or the back legs of the chair (palms facing out).

⊃ Straighten the legs and push the feet and heels against the wall ❷.

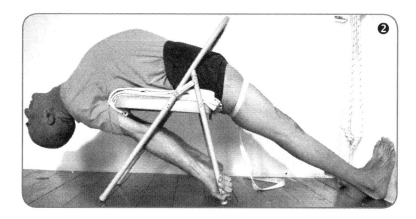

⮑ If you find it hard to straighten the legs, use a block to raise the heels ❸.

⮑ After staying in the pose for several minutes, take the arms out and hold the elbows beyond the head. Keeping the shoulders rolled back, extend the elbows and lower them down ❹.

⮑ You can then stretch the arms, placing the back of the hands on the floor ❺.

Gradually, you can slide out of the chair (towards the head) and work on different latitudes of the back. The feet will be drawn away from the wall.

If possible, bend the elbows around the front legs of the chair and place the crown of the head on the floor (or on a folded blanket). This will bring you closer to the classic pose ❻.

Staying in the pose, one realizes why B.K.S. Iyengar writes the following in *Light on Yoga*: "This exhilarating pose keeps the spine sound and healthy while the chest expands fully... The pose has a very soothing effect on the mind, so that the emotionally disturbed find it a great boon". The pose also gently stimulates the heart and improves blood circulation.

No wonder the use of the chair in this pose is so common (in some of Prashant Iyengar's classes in Pune, this pose is practiced for over an hour).

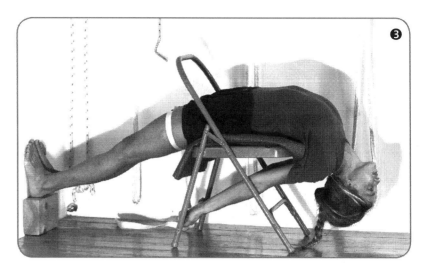

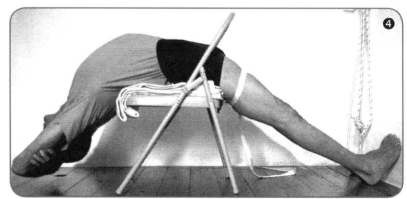

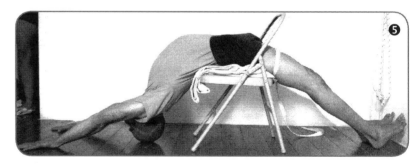

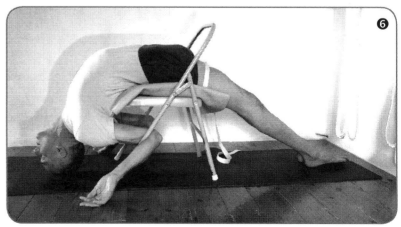

More Variations of Viparita Dandasana with the chair
The following variations enhance some specific effects of the same pose:

1. Lifting the pelvis with a belt
A belt can be used to lift the pelvis higher:
- Place an un-buckled belt across the chair seat.
- Sit on the chair and wrap the belt around your sacral band.
- Take the two ends of the belt, pass them through the backrest, wrap them around the top bar of the backrest and cross them, so that the belt end coming from your left side is held by your right palm and vice versa ❶.
- Arch the back over the edge of the seat and pull the edges of the belt to lift the pelvis ❷.

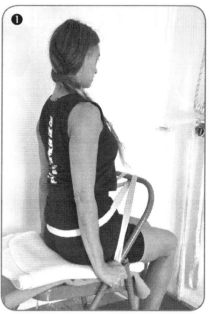

This variation is very gentle and can serve as a nice warm up, especially when back bends were not practiced for a while for some reason (e.g. after delivery or illness).

It is also possible to loop the belt and tighten it around the backrest ❸.
To intensify the back arch and the stretch, straighten your legs and stretch them, move the tail bone further in ❹.

The lift of the pelvis can alleviate lower back aches which some people experience in this pose.

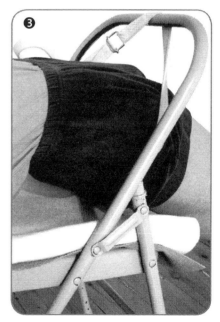

2. **Using a rolled mat**

A rolled sticky mat can be used to increase the movement and to alleviate some problems in the pose. Three alternatives are shown below:

i) Support the sacral-coccyx band.

  ➲ Place a rolled sticky mat lengthwise, aligned with the spine under the buttocks ❶.

This can alleviate pressure on the lower back. A helper can gently pull the rolled mat to lengthen the sacral area.

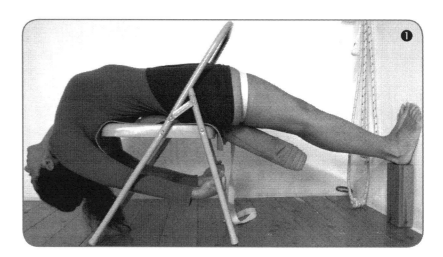

ii) Support the chest.

  ➲ Place the rolled mat widthwise under the mid-chest area ❷.

iii) Support the lumbar.

  ➲ Place the rolled mat widthwise under the mid-lumbar area ❸.

This can alleviate pressure in the lumbar region.

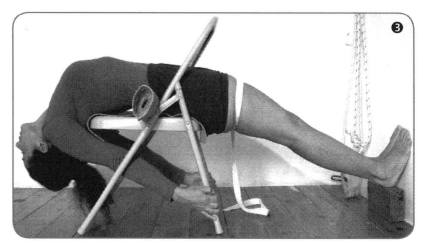

3. Placing weight on the thighs

One action you need to do in the pose is to move the front thighs back and make them heavy while elongating the back of the legs toward the wall. To demonstrate this effect, a helper can stand on the practitioner's thighs. This is very pleasant since the extra weight on the thighs helps to open the chest (when I teach this pose I find myself stepping from one student's thighs to another).

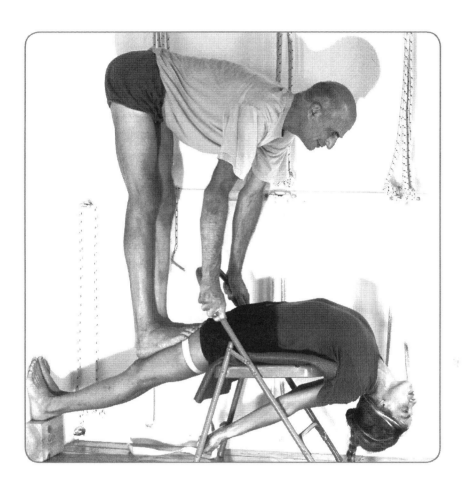

Sliding out of the chair

This section is intended for advanced practitioners.

i) Slide toward *Chakra Bandhasana* (LOY, Pl. 524).

- ⮑ Slide a little further out of the chair until the head touches the floor (if needed, place a folded blanket on the floor).

- ⮑ Bend the elbows and grip the front legs of the chair **❶**. If you find it hard to reach the chair's legs, you can loop a belt around them and hold the belt instead (not shown).

ii) Slide toward *Kapotasana* (LOY, Pl. 512).

- ⮑ Bend the knees and place the front ankles or shins on the back rung of the chair.

- ⮑ Insert the arms in between the front legs of the chair and grip the ankles **❷**, or interlock the arms above the head **❸**.

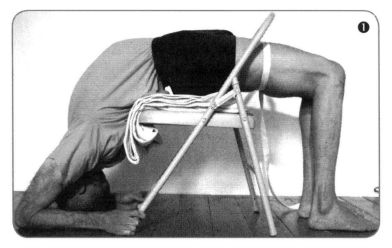

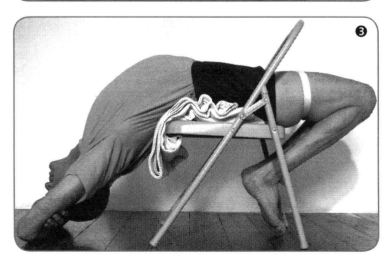

⮥ If possible, bend the knees further and place the metatarsals (top sides of the feet) on the front rung ❹.

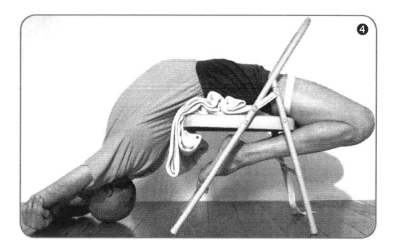

iii) Move into *Urdhva Dhanurasana* (LOY, Pl. 482).

⮥ From *Viparita Dandasana*, bend the legs and place the heels on the back legs of the chair.

⮥ Place the palms on the floor, as close as possible to the front legs of the chair.

⮥ Lift the trunk up from the seat and move the pubic area toward the backrest. If possible, lift the chair with the pubic bone.

iv) Practice *Eka Pada Viparita Dandasana* (LOY, Pl. 521).

➲ Move out of the chair. Sit on the chair and insert only one leg under the backrest as shown in *Dwi Pada Viparita Dandasana.* (see page 105.) Place the other leg over the backrest, folded at the knee.

➲ Use a belt to pull the heel of the lifted leg then straighten both legs.

➲ First, stretch the lifted leg vertically up ❶, then you can stretch your hamstrings further by pulling the lifted leg toward your body ❷.

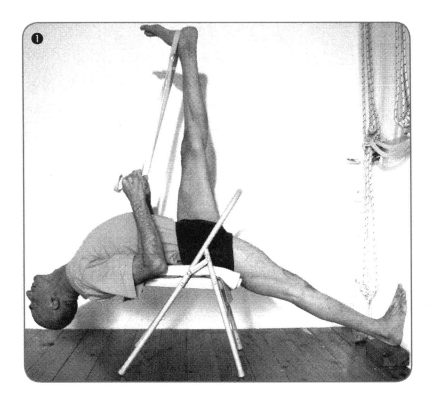

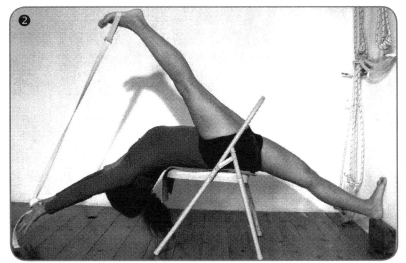

Folding the legs

You can bring the legs to *Padmasana* (lotus pose) on the chair. The interlock of *Padmasana* keeps the legs from opening.

However, for *Baddha Konasana* you will need a belt.

⮕ Loop the belt around the backrest.

⮕ Bend the legs to *Baddha Konasana* and support the feet with the belt ❶.

⮕ Lie on the seat and arch back ❷.

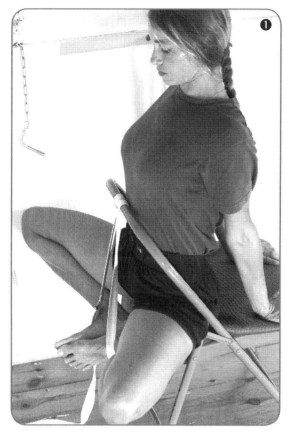

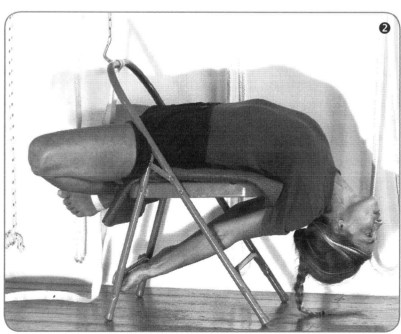

Coming out of the pose

The common way of coming out of chair *Dwi Pada Viparita Dandasana* is to bend the knees, inhale and then lift the chest and head to a sitting position. As an alternative, which I personally find much more suitable try the following:

⮑ Bend the knees and insert the feet under the back rung. Extend the toes backwards ❶.

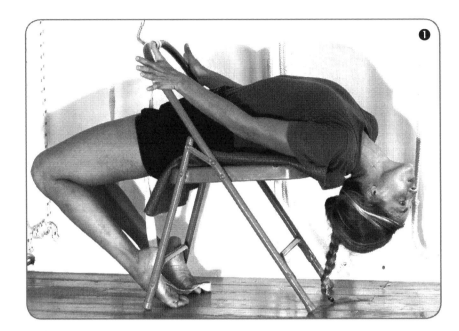

⮑ Slide down from the chair until the knees reach the floor. Lie back on the seat and hold the elbows ❷.

This is supported *Kapotasana*. It is very relaxing to rest on the chair in this way, breathing into the open chest.

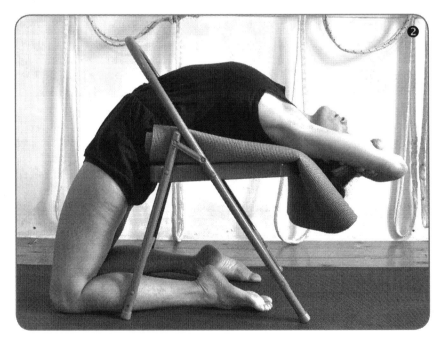

⮑ As you raise the torso from the seat, draw the chair's backrest with you and bring it over in front of the body as you sit on the heels. Rest the back against the tilted seat ❸.

⮑ You can then twist to the sides, using the legs of the chair ❹.

Variation 2: Upper body inserted under the backrest

It is possible to practice *Dwi Pada Viparita Dandasana* on the chair from the opposite side of the chair. This is especially preferable if you plan to move from *Dwi pada* to *Eka Pada Viparita Dandasana.*

⮺ Place the chair at the appropriate distance from the wall, with its seat toward the wall. Put a folded sticky mat on the seat and possibly a folded blanket for cushioning.

⮺ Loop a belt around the backrest and let it hang.

⮺ Sit on the floor with your back to the seat, legs toward the wall. Lie back on the seat and insert the arms through the hollow backrest, then the head, and finally, the chest.

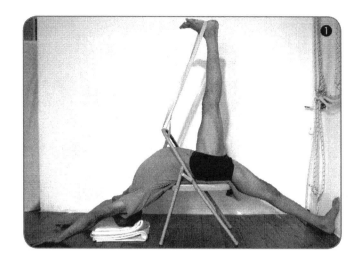

⮺ Arch the back and stretch the legs with the feet pushing against the wall.

⮺ Now, to continue into *Eka Pada Viparita Dandasan*, bend one leg, loop the prepared belt around its heel and stretch the leg up against the resistance of the belt (tighten or loosen the belt as needed). This is supported *Eka Pada Viparita Dandasana I* (LOY, Pl. 521) ❶.

You can also lift both legs to *Viparita Karani.* Clearly, it is easier to raise the leg into the *Eka Pada* variation when you enter the chair in this manner, since the backrest does not get in the way. In addition, the belt is stretched against the backrest, keeping the leg active, while enabling you to stretch the arms over the head or to interlock the fingers around the back of the head (not shown).

From there, continue toward *Eka Pada Viparita Dandasana II* (LOY, Pl. 523).

⮺ Bend the lower leg and place the back of the foot above the front rung. Continue using the belt for the lifted leg.

⮺ Bend the elbows and grip the back legs of the chair ❷.

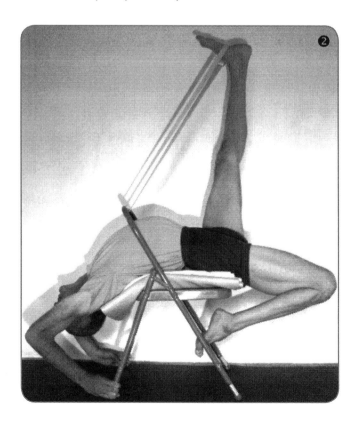

◌ Now, use the belt to perform *Dwi Pada Viparita Baddha Konasana*. Adjust the length of the belt so that the belt supports the feet at seat level ❸.

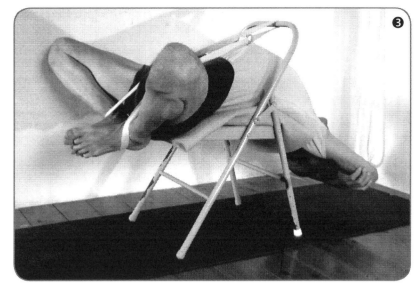

◌ Finally, interlock the legs to *Padmasana* and hold the arms at the elbows. This is *Dwi Pada Viparita Padmasana* ❹.

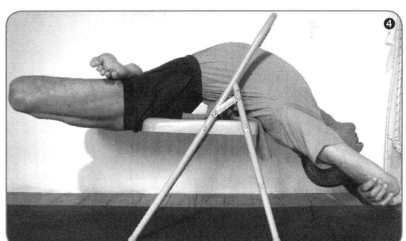

◌ To come out of the pose, release the legs' interlock and slide down toward the legs until the knees are on the floor (if you need, you can prepare a bolster in advance to support the knees).

Ustrasana

The chair is used here to support the back in order to increase the chest opening. It also enables to stay longer in the pose.

Variation 1: Supported by the seat (with 2 bolsters)

⮑ Place two bolsters on the seat. Kneel with your back to the seat and slide the shins and feet beneath it.

⮑ Press the shins, arch backwards and rest your back on the bolsters. If you are tall, the head will be supported by the backrest ❶; otherwise, use a rolled blanket to support the back of the neck. Hold the backrest ❷.

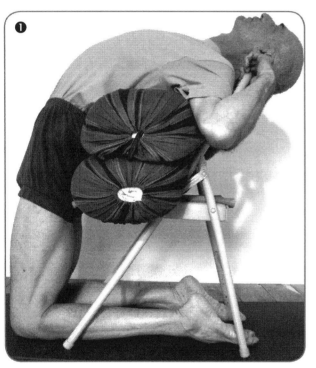

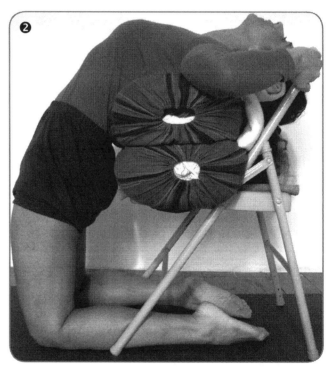

To use the wall:

⮑ Place the chair with its backrest toward the wall at the appropriate distance from it.

⮑ Extend the arms over the head and push the finger tips against the wall ❸.

Variation 2: Supported by the backrest

↪ Kneel with the back facing the backrest.

↪ Arch back and rest your back on the backrest. The backrest should support the back just below the shoulder blades ❶. You can tilt the chair to adjust the height of the backrest according to your needs ❷.

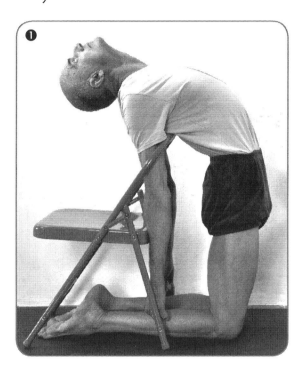

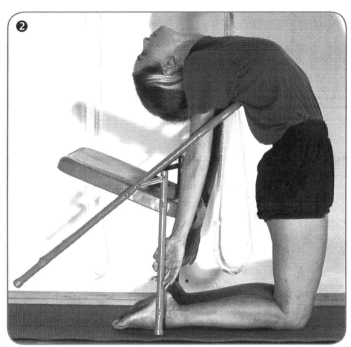

You can also do it facing the wall as in ❸.

The wall is used as a reference. Push the pubic bone against it to ensure the verticality of the thighs, and to help move the tail bone in.

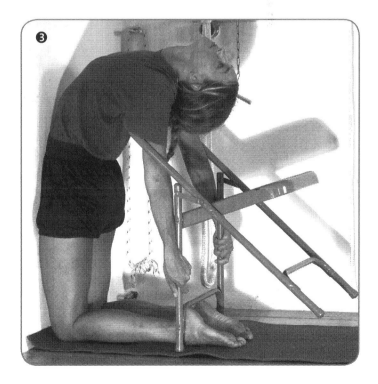

You can also fold the chair and use it against the wall as follows:

- ➲ Fold the chair and place its legs against the wall. The seat of the chair should face down.

- ➲ Kneel with your back to the wall in front of the chair. Place the backrest against the back. The backrest should lean against the sacral girdle ❹ or the top lumbar area ❺.

- ➲ Unfold the chair slightly and insert the arms between the backrest and the seat.

- ➲ Arch back into the pose and place the palms on the soles of the feet, as in the classic pose (LOY, Pl. 41).

The placement of the chair against the wall keeps it stable and creates an excellent fulcrum for the back bending action.

Variation 3: Kneeling facing the chair

⮑ Kneel facing the chair, so that the pelvic area is pressed firmly against the front edge of the seat.

⮑ Hold the seat and start curving the back ❶.

⮑ Keep pushing the pelvis (or front groins if you are tall) against the seat and move the arms behind your back. Place the palms on the soles of the feet as in the classic pose ❷.

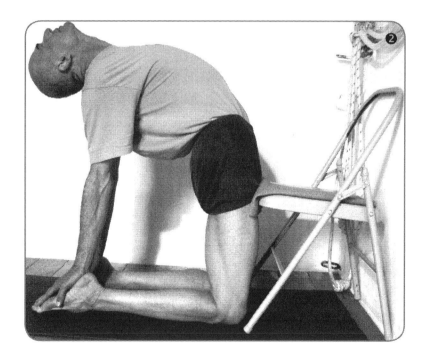

Urdhva Dhanurasana

Urdva Dhanurasana (LOY, Pl. 482) is a challenge for many students. The chair can be used in a variety of ways to lift the body into the back arch, and stay there more comfortably. The following variations serve to:

1. Prepare for the pose and facilitate entering into it
2. Support the pose for a longer period
3. Alter the geometry of the pose, to achieve different effects.

Variation 1: Preparation, lying on a bolster

↪ Place the chair with its side facing the wall, about 75 cm (30 inches) from the wall. Put a bolster widthwise on the seat (parallel to the backrest).

↪ Lie on the bolster with your head toward the wall. The bolster should support the back and buttocks.

↪ Keep the knees bent and stretch the arms over the head to touch the wall with the palms or finger tips ❶.

↪ Once you get accustomed to the back arch, straighten the legs one by one, extend them, and push the floor with the heels ❷.

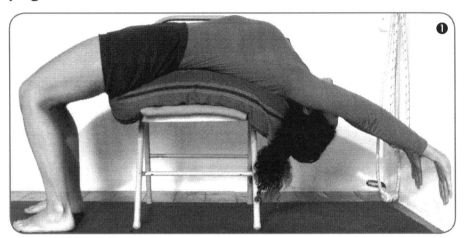

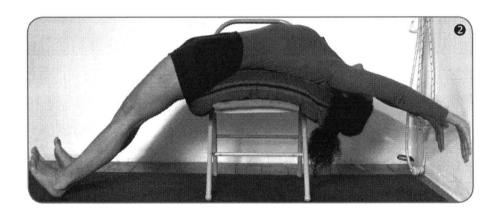

In case you need a wider support for the back, use two chairs. Position the chairs one against the other and place two or three bolsters on theirs seats.

This preparatory variation opens the chest and helps to create movement in the shoulders. It is a good warm-up for the actual pose. People who are not ready to do the independent pose will find this variation a refreshing substitute.

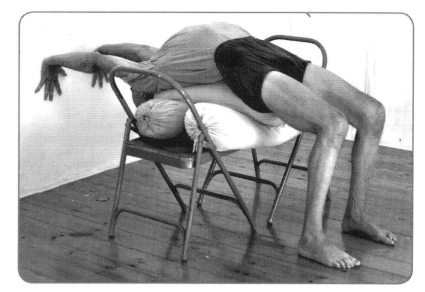

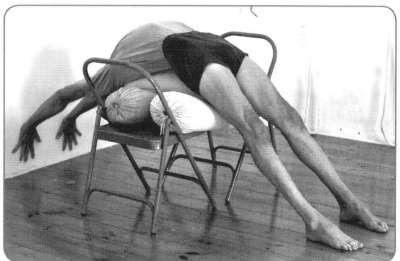

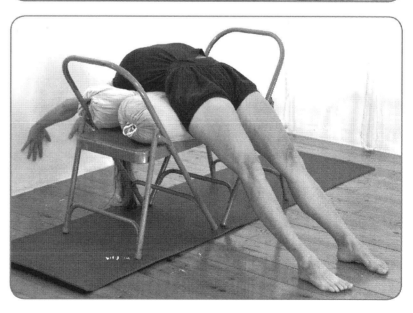

Variation 2: Using the chair to enter the pose

⮑ Place the chair with its back against the wall. Place a bolster in front of the chair.

⮑ Sit on the bolster then lean back on the front edge of the seat ❶.

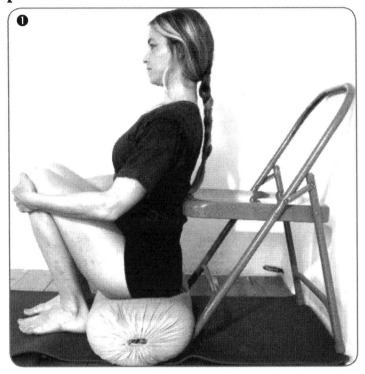

⮑ Lift yourself, lie back on the seat and hold the backrest ❷.

⮑ Now, lift further and place the top of the head on the seat ❸.

⮑ Then, move the hands to the wall and push the wall to lift up. Straighten the arms and use the support of the wall to stay in this arched pose ❹.

⮑ To come down, bend the arms and knees and lower yourself down to the chair. Then, sit on the bolster in front of the chair.

Using the chair in this way, it is quite easy to enter the pose. We asked the photographer (a beginner student) to do it, and he lifted himself up into the pose with no difficulty.

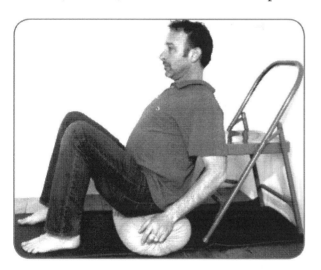

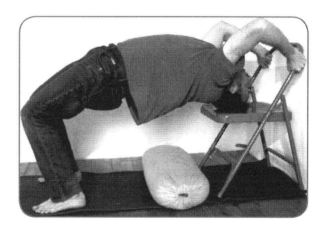

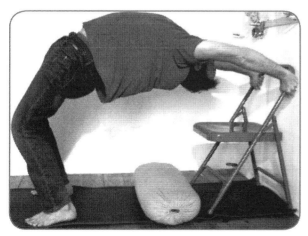

Another way to lift up into *Urdhva Dhanurasana*, using an inverted chair, is shown in the following photos:

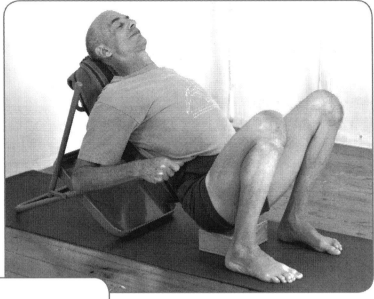

Variation 3: Back supported on the chair

This is yet another easy way to enter the pose and stay in it comfortably.

⮎ Place the chair with its back facing the wall, at a distance of about 1 meter (3.5 feet) from the wall. Sit on the chair and place a bolster or two between your back and the backrest ❶.

⮎ Arch back then lift yourself up. Stretch the arms over the head to reach the wall.

⮎ Stay with your back supported by the backrest and the bolsters while pushing the wall with the hands ❷.

In the beginning, it is safer to have somebody hold the chair to prevent it from tilting back; however, advanced practitioners can easily do this variation on their own, without bolsters.

↪ Place the chair with its back facing the wall at a distance of about 1 meter (3.5 feet) from the wall. Sit on the chair and place a folded sticky mat on the backrest.

↪ Place the heels on the front legs of the chair. This will prevent the chair from tilting.

↪ Lift yourself up from the chair while arching backwards; use the top of the backrest as a support for the mid-back area. Stretch the arms over the head and reach the wall ❶.

↪ Now, arch further and move the palms down the wall, one after the other ❷.

This variation increases the flexibility of the upper back and shoulders, enabling a deeper arching of the upper body.

Variation 4: Pelvis supported on the chair

↪ Place the chair with its back facing the wall, at a distance of about 1 meter (3.5 feet) from the wall. Place a folded sticky mat on the backrest and a bolster on the seat.

↪ Stand in between the chair and the wall, facing the wall.

↪ Place the sacral area on the backrest, taking the tail bone deep in. If needed, lift the heels ❶ or place the feet on blocks.

↪ Arch back over the backrest and place the head on the bolster. If you are tall, you may not need the bolster on the seat.

↪ If possible, extend the arms and hold the front legs of the chair ❷.

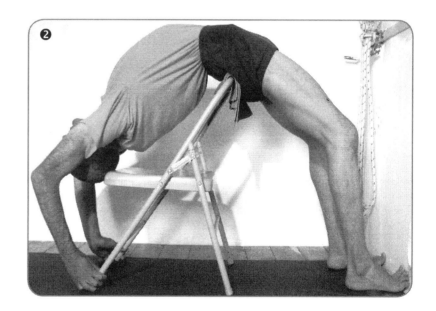

A helper can assist in stretching the arms and increasing the arch.

↪ The helper places one foot on the seat. After arching back, the practitioner grasps the helper's leg. The helper gently pulls the practitioner arms while turning the triceps muscles inward toward his/her face.

This variation increases the flexibility of the lower back and helps to keep the tail bone and sacrum well lifted. Note: the sticky mat may be replaced by a bolster if more height is required for supporting the back ❸.

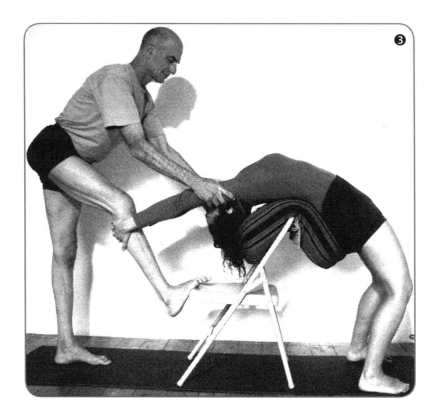

Variation 5: Catching the legs of the chair

This is the first variation in which you attempt to enter the pose from the floor.

- Place the chair with its seat facing the wall.
- Lie on your back, head close to the chair, and grip its back legs. Push the chair a little toward the wall. The chair will slide and fold slightly until being stopped by the wall ❶.

- Lift yourself and place the crown of the head on the floor. Now, press the arms and head to tuck in the shoulder blades and arch the upper back.

- Pushing the hands against the chair legs, move the body away from it and straighten the arms. Turn the upper arms from outside in (triceps muscles rolling toward the face) and make sure the elbows are kept absolutely straight.

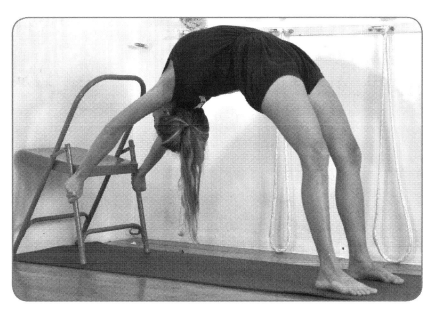

◌ Now, walk the feet slightly in and, without bending the elbows, move the chest closer to the wall.

Holding the chair provides anchoring for the hands. It also provides a raised support for the palms and keeps them turned in, both of which help the lifting and the turning of the arms.

If you find it difficult to lift from the floor, you can lie with the back on a bolster.

This variation can also be done with the back of the chair facing the wall; however, you should be careful to push the legs of the chair strongly **downward** in order to prevent the chair from sliding and folding against the wall.

◌ Place the chair with its back facing the wall.
◌ Hold the front legs of the chair and push DOWN to lift yourself up. Place the crown of the head on the floor. Lift your shoulder blades ❶.
◌ Lift further to place the back of the head on the seat.
◌ Lower the palms toward the floor, grasp the legs of the chair ❷, or place the palms on the floor ❸.

◌ After holding the pose

for a few minutes, move the palms to the seat and push to straighten the elbows ❹.

Placing the head on the seat as in ❷ and ❸ has a special effect on the opening of the chest.

Once you place the palms on the seat and straighten the arms, as in ❹, the geometry of the pose changes. The load on the arms is reduced significantly, enabling you to lift the chest and stay in the pose with less effort.

Variation 6: Feet on the chair

This variation changes the geometry of the pose in a different way.

- ⮌ Place the chair next to the wall, with its back facing the wall. Place a sticky mat on the seat.
- ⮌ Lie on the floor, your legs close to the chair, and place the feet on the seat.

- ⮌ Push yourself up and place the crown of the head on the floor ❶.
- ⮌ Inhale, then exhale and push further to straighten the arms ❷.
- ⮌ If stable, you can lift one leg and approach *Eka Pada Urdhva Dhanurasana* (LOY, Pl. 501) ❸.

Lifting yourself up with the feet raised on the seat is quite straining for the arms, but once you are up, it is easier to keep the elbows straight, to move the shoulder blades in, and to open the chest.

Because of the high support of the feet, the pelvis (pubic bone) is horizontal, so there is absolutely no tension in the lower abdomen. It remains soft and relaxed; hence, women who practice *Urdhva Dhanurasana* regularly can stay in this variation during (normal) pregnancy, or even after a cesarean delivery (only after recovering from the operation, of course).

However, pushing into the pose in these conditions is not appropriate, thus the presence of a helper is required to help you get into and out of the pose ❹ ❺.

Urdhva Dhanurasana II

Plates 483 to 486 in LOY show how to arch back from *Tadasana* to *Urdhava Danurasana;* BKS Iyengar writes there: "while learning the pose this way it is helpful to use a friend or a wall." However, the chair can also be used in the following way:

➲ Stand with your legs apart at pelvis-width in front of the back of the chair. Hold the backrest.

➲ Lift your chest and start arching back. Push the chair to lift the chest and to move your shoulder blades into the body ❶.

➲ Use the support of the chair to arch further while maintaining the lift of the chest ❷.

➲ If possible, bend the knees slightly and place the palms on the seat ❸.

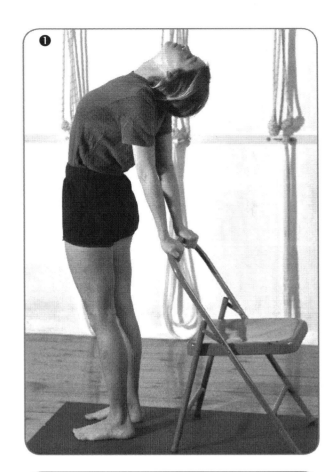

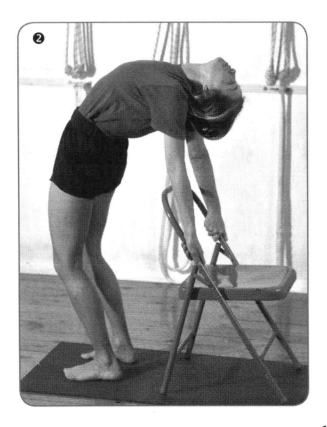

Dropping to Dwi Pada Viparita Dandasana

Advanced practitioners enter this pose by dropping back from *Sirsasana* (LOY, Pl. 517-520). This requires balance, control, and flexibility. When learning, the chair can be used as an intermediate landing for the feet.

As a preparation, you may want to open the shoulders. You can do it in the following way:

- ➲ Hold a block to maintain the palms at shoulder width.
- ➲ Kneel near the chair and place the elbows on the backrest.
- ➲ Create movement in the shoulders by moving the sternum bone away from the arms. Avoid pushing the sternum toward the floor.

Now, to drop into the pose:

- ➲ Perform *Sirsasana* at the appropriate distance from the chair, with your back facing the seat.
- ➲ Bend the knees and point the feet to the chair ❶.
- ➲ Keep lifting the shoulders and tucking the shoulder blades in while arching back.
- ➲ Arch further back, until the feet land on the seat ❷. Lift the shoulder blades way up.

In the learning process, fear may arise out of concern of missing the chair. A helper can secure the landing and correct the positioning of the chair if needed ❸ ❹.

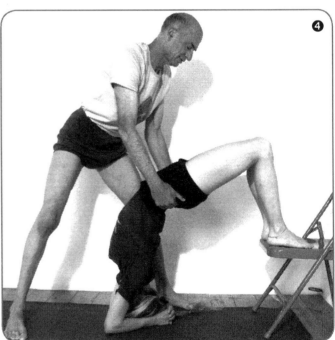

Vrschikasana I

This is an advanced pose (LOY, Pl. 536-7); the chair can help you to work towards it. Dropping into the pose is similar to that of *Dwi Pada Viparita Dandasana* (see page 137), but here you start from *Pincha Mayurasana* rather than from *Sirsasana*.

- Hold the legs of the chair and go up to *Pincha Mayurasana*.
- Bend the knees and point the feet toward the chair.
- Keep lifting the shoulders and pushing the shoulder blades in while arching back.
- Arch further back, until the feet land on the backrest ❶.
- Then lower the feet down to the seat. Keep pushing the chest forward and walk the feet toward your back ❷.

Eka Pada Rajakapotasana I

The chair can help you work toward this advanced pose (LOY, Pl. 542) in two ways:

Variation 1: Chair in front

To work with the left leg in front:

- ➲ Place the chair at the appropriate distance from the wall, with its seat facing the wall.
- ➲ Bend the left leg and place it under the chair (you can support the left buttock with a folded blanket).
- ➲ Bend the right leg and place the front shin and foot against the wall.
- ➲ Place the forearms on the seat and push to lift the chest and arch back.

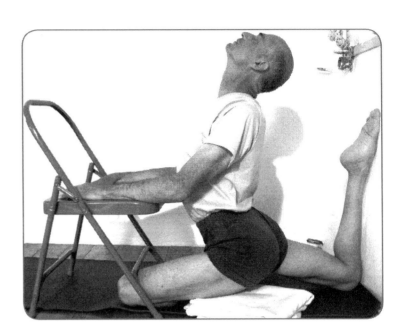

Variation 2: Chair at the back

To work with the left leg in front:

- ➲ Place the chair with its back against the wall. Put a folded mat on the seat and a weight on it (the weight prevents the chair from tilting). Tighten a belt around the backrest.
- ➲ Bend the left leg and put it on the floor in front. Bend the right leg and place the front ankle against the seat.
- ➲ Grip the belt and pull it while lifting the chest and arching back toward the chair ❶.

You may experience difficulty because of the instability of the chair. A helper can sit on the chair to stabilize it and help with your arching by pulling the arms gently.

In ❷, the helper uses his right foot to broaden and lower the right side of the practitioner's pelvis, and uses his left knee to support the practitioner's upper back.

Note: This variation is for advanced practitioners only. The helper should be an experienced Yoga teacher.

Natarajasana

The chair can help you work toward this advanced and elegant pose (LOY, Pl. 590).

To use the chair to support the right knee:

↪ Place the chair at the appropriate distance behind you, with its back facing you. Put a 10 kg (22 pounds) weight on the seat to prevent the chair from tilting.

↪ Loop a belt around your right foot and, while bending slightly forward, use it for lifting the leg up and placing the right knee on the backrest.

↪ With a circular movement, lift the right elbow up. Pull the right foot further up, then lift the chest and arch back.

↪ Now, grip the belt with the left hand too ❶, or stretch the left arm diagonally up.

The support for the back knee should be as high as your pelvis; hence, tall people may need to place folded blankets on the backrest to raise the support ❷.

If you find it hard to keep your balance, stand in front of the wall, and place the left hand on the wall for stability ❸. Alternatively, a helper can sit on the chair and catch your arms ❹.

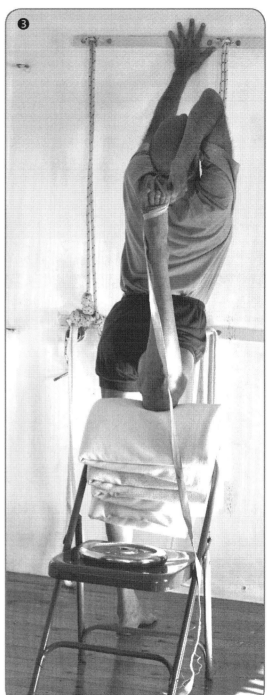

Purvottanasana

The challenge of this pose (LOY, Pl. 171) is to lift both the pelvis and the chest. Lying back on the seat of the chair supports both thus enabling you to stay longer in the pose while fully extending the front of the body.

If the palms do not reach the floor, use blocks (not shown).

Chapter 7: Abdominal –Udara Akunchana Sthiti

Paripurna Navasana

For most people, entering this pose and maintaining it for more than a few seconds is a challenge. Using chairs, you can build up strength and stamina and prepare yourself for the classic pose. Two variations are presented below.

Variation 1: Calves on the chair

⮑ Sit on the floor in front of the chair.

⮑ Place the mid-calf muscles on the front edge of the seat. Hold the seat and pull it against the legs. This will help you open the chest lift the sacrum away from the floor and concave the back ❶.

⮑ Now, release the seat and stretch the arms forward, parallel to the floor. Maintain the concavity of your back while stretching the arms and legs ❷.

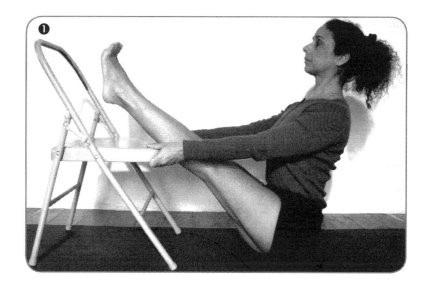

Variation 2: In between two chairs

↪ Place two chairs facing each other at the appropriate distance.

↪ Sit on one chair and place the mid-calves on the other one.

↪ Move the pelvis slightly forward and lower it while pushing the palms against the seat ❶.

↪ Slowly descend until the buttocks rest on the floor. Hold the legs of the chair you are leaning on. Move the shoulders back and concave the back ❷.

↪ Now stretch the arms forward parallel to the floor ❸.

In this variation, the pose is fully supported by the chairs, enabling you to extend its duration. When you feel ready, try to lift the legs off the chair for a few seconds.

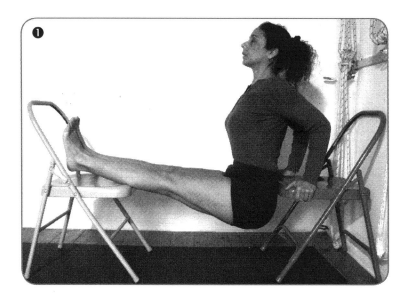

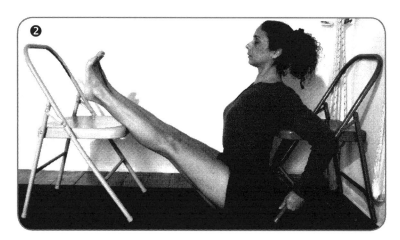

Urdhva Prasarita Padasana

For people with short hamstrings, holding the legs perpendicular to the floor is difficult. They either lower the legs towards the floor or lift the sacral band. Using the chair it is possible to support the sacral band and gradually lengthen the hamstrings until a 90^0 angle can be achieved.

Legs against the chair
- Lie on your back next to the chair.
- Lift your legs up and move the chair so that its back supports the back of your legs. Hold the legs of the chair to stabilize the lower back.
- Lift the buttocks and place the sacrum on the back rung of the chair. Maintain the pose ❶.
- After a while, you can slide down until the sacral band rests on the floor. Continue to support your legs vertically on the chair ❷. Gradually, try to pull the legs away from the chair to increase the engagement of your abdominal muscles.

You may also start by placing the back of the knees on the backrest. Place a blanket to make the backrest thicker and release the shins over it. This is very relaxing; it creates space in the knees and lengthens the ligaments. If you have pain in the ligaments of the knees, this variation may be very helpful in relieving it over time.

Uttana Padasana

In the classic pose (LOY, Pl. 292), the back is arched and the crown of the head rests on the floor; however, to prepare yourself, you can practice it while lying on two chairs as explained below.

- ⮑ Place two chairs facing and touching each other. Place a folded sticky mat on the seats and lay your back on it.
- ⮑ Place yourself so that the mid-sacrum is aligned with the rear edge of one seat.
- ⮑ Hold the backrest of that same chair and lift the legs up 45°. Stretch the legs and keep them tight and joined ❶. If this is difficult, slide slightly toward the head side, so that the entire sacrum will be supported by the chair.
- ⮑ Raise the arms, join the palms and keep the arms parallel to the legs ❷.

If lifting the arms is difficult, you can practice the first stage ❶ until you develop sufficient strength in the abdominal muscles.

Chapter 8: Restorative –Visranta Karaka Sthiti

Supta Virasana

This pose can be practiced actively (LOY, Pl. 96), or with support. When done with support, this is one of the best *asanas* for deep relaxation and restoration. It also stretches and massages the front thighs and improves the flexibility and health of the knees. For some people a bolster is not sufficient and they need higher support in order to stay comfortably in the pose. An inverted chair provides such support, thus enabling almost everyone to enjoy the pose.

⮑ Invert the chair and place a bolster on its horizontal rungs (which now face upward). Place a folded blanket or two in front of the chair.

⮑ Sit in *Virasana* on the blankets then recline the trunk back to lie on the bolster. Place a folded blanket under the head and neck.

⮑ Hold the elbows above the head and stay in the pose.

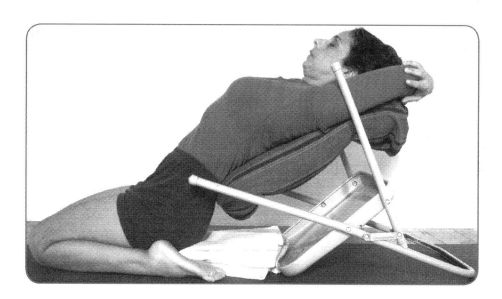

Salamba Purvottanasana

This is a restorative variation of *Purvottanasana* (LOY, Pl. 171) (*Salamba* means "with support").

⮑ Place the chair with its backrest about 1 meter (3.5 feet) away from the wall. Place a second chair opposite the first one to create a platform. Spread a sticky mat across the two seats and then two bolsters on top. Slide the top bolster slightly further away from the wall to create a step for the lower back. Insert a block under the head side of the top bolster and prepare a folded blanket as a head rest.

⮑ Pass the legs under the backrest and sit on the lower bolster. Stretch the legs and push the feet against the wall.

⮑ The buttock bones should rest on the bottom bolster, while the upper buttock area should be supported by the top bolster.

⮑ Lie back on the bolsters. Rest the head and back of the neck on the folded blanket. Hold the elbows above the head ❶ or spread the arms sideways ❷.

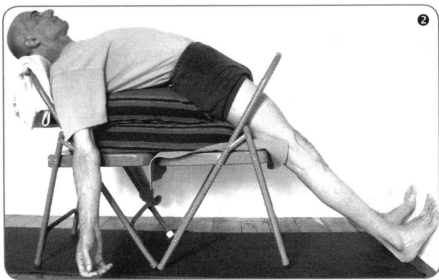

Setu Bandha Sarvangasana

↻ Place the chair with its backrest at the appropriate distance from the wall and place a sticky mat on its seat. Place a block next to the wall.

↻ Place two bolsters on the floor in front of the chair and prepare an additional blanket or two near the seat.

↻ Insert the legs under the backrest. Tighten a belt around the upper thighs. Stretch the legs and place the heels on the block and the soles of the feet against the wall.

↻ Lie on the seat and arch back. Rest the shoulders, back of the neck, and back of the head on the support. Using the blankets, adjust the height of the head support as needed for comfort.

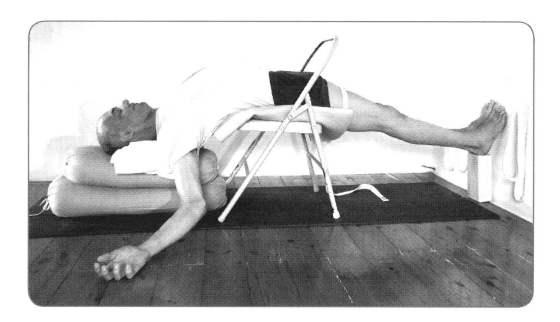

Salamba Viparita Karani

Viparita Karani is a very effective restorative pose. In this variation there is further relaxation of the abdominal organs.

⮑ Place two bolsters, one on top of the other, in front of the chair. (if needed, place a rolled blanket between the bolsters and the chair in order to maintain a narrow gap, not shown).

⮑ Raise the level of the seat using foam blocks and blankets. The height of the seat should enable your shins to rest horizontally when lying with your buttocks on the bolsters.

⮑ Prepare a folded blanket for head and shoulder support.

⮑ Sit on the bolsters with your side to the chair and roll into the pose. The back of the pelvis and the lumbar should lie comfortably on the bolsters and the buttock bones should extend slightly beyond the edge of the bolsters. The upper legs should be perpendicular and the lower legs horizontal.

⮑ There should be no load on the shoulders; rather, the chest should be well lifted. The energy of the body should move from the shoulders to the lower abdomen and from the legs to the lower abdomen.

⮑ Relax the abdomen completely, and stay in the pose quietly for a few minutes.

Savasana

Two ways of using the chair in *Savasana* are presented.

Variation 1: Shins on the chair

⮕   Place the chair at one end of the mat. Lie down into *Savasana* with the shins resting on the seat.

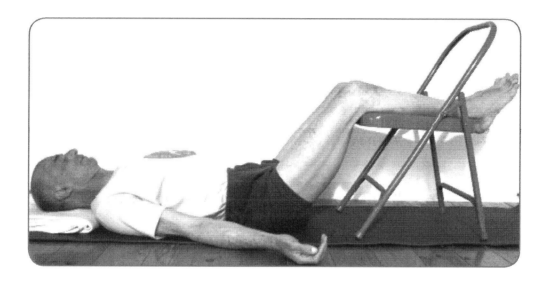

The lift of the legs creates length in the lower back, which becomes flat and relaxed. This alleviates lower back pain created by jamming in this area. It also softens and relaxes the abdominal organs.

Variation 2: Head supported

- Tie a belt around the seat of the chair and let it hang near the floor. Place the chair near one end of the mat with its side to the mat.
- Lie on your back, head under the chair.
- Insert the head through the loose belt and rest the back of the head on it. Adjust the length of the loop so that the head is slightly raised from the floor and the back of the neck is elongated.

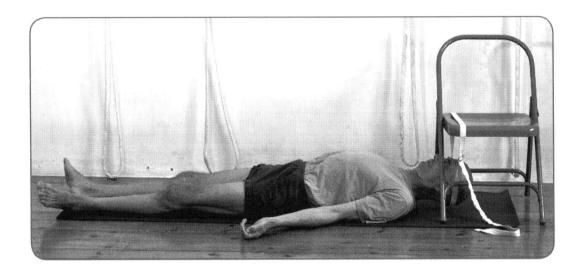

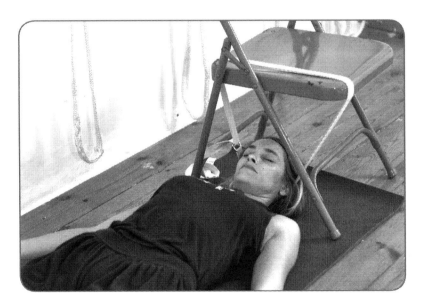

The support for the head induces a relaxed, floating sensation. The back of the neck is elongated and there is a feeling of openness in the inner ears. This variation helps to alleviate dizziness.

Final Words

"Yoga is for all. Nobody should be denied the opportunity to experience its benevolence. It is this thought that impelled me to think of all these props" – this is how BKS Iyengar describes his motivation for developing the props.

Mr. Iyengar has created numerous props for the benefit of one's Yoga practice in the course of his many years of *Sadhana*. Some are his original design, others adapted from household objects, such as the chair.

It is indeed fascinating to discover the variety of uses that a simple furniture can provide. However, I once again wish to stress that props are only an aid for learning the physical and mental effects that *asana* practice can bring about. In addition, while the variations presented in this guide can give you hours of joyful and interesting practice, they are by no means exhaustive. Feel free to explore and invent other ways of using the chair in your own Yoga practice.

I hope that you will enjoy this process as much as I have!
Eyal Shifroni,
March, 2013

Appendix: A chair for all – a gentle practice sequence

The presentation in this guide is arranged by "families of *asanas*". However, the full effect of Yoga practice is very much affected by the specific sequence followed in a particular session. Such sequencing must be chosen according to the purpose and intention of the session.

This appendix presents an example of such a sequence using the chair. This particular sequence is intended as a recreational practice for everyone. You can practice it, or parts of it, at all times and almost anywhere, even at your work desk. This sequence is also adequate for elderly people and for those suffering from movement limitations.

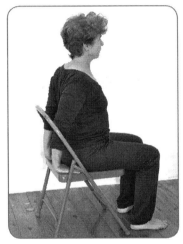

1. *Tadasana* on chair
Push the seat to lift

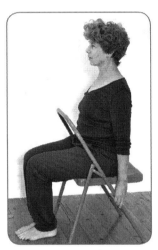

2. *Tadasana* on chair
Pull the chair's legs

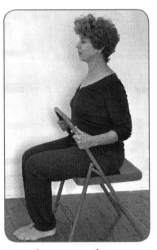

3. *Tadasana* on chair
Pull the backrest

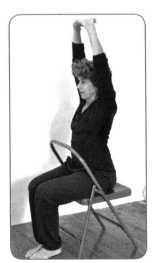

4. *Urdhva Baddhaguliyasana* on chair

5. *Paschima Baddhaguliyasana* bend forward

6. *Garudasana* on chair

7. *Utkatasana* on chair

8. *Kurmasana* stage 1

9. *Kurmasana* stage 2

10. *Paschimottanasana*

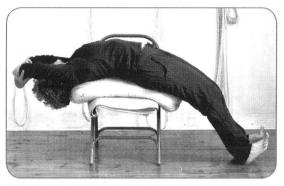

11. *Padmasana* preparation stage 1

12. *Padmasana* preparation stage 2

13. *Dwi Pada Viparita Dandasana* arms above head

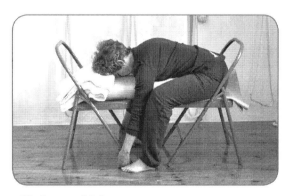

14. *Dwi Pada Viparita Dandasana* arms under chair

15. *Pavana Muktasana*

16. *Parsva Pavana Muktasana*

17. *Pasasna*

18. *Maricyasana III*

19. *Maricyasana III*
back view

20. *Parsva Upavistha Konasana*

21. *Bharadvajasana I*
block between legs

22. *Bharadvajasana I*
Block between pelvis and chair

23. *Salamba Sarvangasana*

24. *Baddha Konasana* in
Sarvangasana

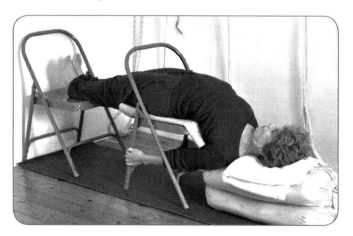

25. *Setu Bandha Sarvangasana*

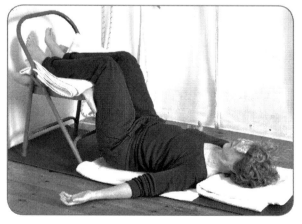

26. *Savasana*

Index

Made in the USA
Lexington, KY
28 August 2014

Made in the USA
Monee, IL,
18 September 2020